CHAPTERS OF EXPERIENCE

Also by Gordon O. Taylor

THE PASSAGES OF THOUGHT

Chapters of Experience

Studies in 20th Century American Autobiography

Gordon O. Taylor

St. Martin's Press   New York

© Gordon O. Taylor 1983

All rights reserved. For information, write:
St. Martin's Press, Inc., 175 Fifth Avenue, New York, NY 10010
Printed in Hong Kong
First published in the United States of America in 1983

ISBN 0–312–12977–7

Library of Congress Cataloging in Publication Data

Taylor, Gordon O.
   Chapters of experience.

   Includes bibliographical references and index.
   Contents: Of Adams and Aquarius: Henry Adams
and Norman Mailer — Chapters of experience: Henry
James — Voices from the veil: W. E. B. DuBois to
Malcolm X — [etc.]
   1. American prose literature — 20th
century — History and criticism.
2. Autobiography.   3. Authors, American — 20th
century — Biography.   I. Title.
PS366.A88T39   1983   813′.5′09 [B]   82–10681
ISBN 0–312–12977–7

For Jonathan Douglas Taylor

Contents

Preface

'Autobiography has been important in this country,' wrote James M. Cox in a still-seminal essay of 1971 entitled 'Autobiography and America.' The understatement was deliberate, and in context effective, for it focused attention on the problem of relationship between the past importance of the autobiographical impulse in 'classical' American literature, and the forms of new alignment and alliance among autobiography, historiography, reportage and the novel which have emerged in this century. This book is an effort to describe some of these new forms of literary alignment and alliance; to chart portions of a current in American writing in which imaginative and documentary modes are increasingly intermingled; to examine aspects of the interplay between 'classical' continuities in such writing and the ways in which it constitutes a pattern of original response to shifting cultural conditions.

Several valuable approaches to the general subject of autobiography in America, or studies of the genre in other cultures with important implications for the American case, have appeared since 1971, among them James Olney's *Metaphors of Self: The Meaning of Autobiography*, Jeffrey Mehlman's *A Structural Study of Autobiography*, Elizabeth Bruss's *Autobiographical Acts: The Changing Situation of a Literary Genre*, Thomas Cooley's *Educated Lives: The Rise of Modern Autobiography in America*, Mutlu Konuk Blasing's *The Art of Life: Studies in American Autobiography*, and Thomas G. Couser's *American Autobiography: The Prophetic Mode*. But Cox's essay has nevertheless, in certain respects bearing centrally on the concerns of this study, not been superseded as a statement of the situation regarding a large and still growing body of twentieth-century material. In tracing a development in American personal narrative from Franklin through Thoreau and Whitman to Henry Adams and Gertrude

Stein, Cox reaffirms a view generally held, before and since: that these are 'central and not peripheral writers, are indeed classic American writers in the sense that their acts of imagination in the form of autobiography are unforgettable imaginative experience.' But the more urgently interesting feature of the discussion is the felt need, more than the fully enacted effort, to provide 'some sense of a present' to consider along with the past developments surveyed. Cox seeks further definition of a 'present' state of American autobiographical affairs as a vantage point from which to assess the historical process, and toward which to view that process as tending. Yet he also senses in this problem of the 'present' a newly insistent subject in itself, requiring to be understood in terms of discontinuity as well as continuity with the past, and calling for reformulations in critical vocabulary and purpose:

> Autobiography and confessional writing are now receiving much more critical attention than they used to, and not merely because criticism has exhausted the other genres and is now moving in on a relatively virgin field. For something has happened to the whole idea of literature in the last ten years. To remember that novelists such as Truman Capote and Norman Mailer have in *In Cold Blood* and *The Armies of the Night* challenged the distinction between nonfiction and fiction; to be reminded that biography and autobiography are more marketable products than fiction; to realize that *The Autobiography of Malcolm X* is somehow one of the great imaginative works of the last decade; . . . to reflect upon all this is to begin to acknowledge that much more has happened than a mere opportunistic exploitation of a neglected field.[1]

In essence if not in every detail, this would seem a decade later to be taken generally for granted. But the emergent issue Cox recognizes in his own sense of his essay as a 'glimpse of the subject,' and in his deliberately provisional assumptions and choice of terms, is still very much in the process of emerging on the American literary scene. 'Something has happened' to our notions of narrative genre. *The Autobiography of Malcolm X* is 'somehow' a considerable work of the imagination despite its indirect authorship. To reflect on such things is to 'begin to acknowledge' the importance of questions – descriptive, critical, historical, theoretical – suggested by such exploratory phrasing. Such phrasing also suggests, and Cox in effect urges, that a good deal more reflection, at close descriptive range, on the detailed characteristics of such narrative phenomena themselves ought perhaps to precede, or at least to accompany, efforts at definitive critical assessment or exhaustive historical or theoretical explanation.

Something *has* happened in relatively recent times to the relationship between the documentary and the imaginative in American writing, something importantly and perhaps uniquely accessible in personal narrative as a locus of such change. The changes so apparent in the 1960s, however, have become apparent over a longer period, emerging as obvious lines of literary force around the turn of the twentieth century, while in some ways still deeply rooted in the past. These lines of force radiate, more than they constitute a linear development, into and by now substantially through the century, their energies still active and their patterns of narrative effect still being discerned. It remains to determine the nature of this process in more detail, and to place in mutually revealing relationship with one another a broader range of twentieth-century works in which it representatively occurs. *The Autobiography of Malcolm X*, to continue the example, *does* accumulate imaginative power and summon aesthetic response, although one may not wish to have it stand alone for the full range of modern autobiographical works difficult to reconcile with traditional ideas of the genre. It remains to develop terms in which to account for this, as in the third chapter of this study, and thus to place the book in a context. Scholars *have* begun to acknowledge the existence and extent of new problems in American literary history and criticism posed by literary phenomena as yet incompletely acknowledged, because incompletely assimilable into established structures of historical analysis, generic classification or critical evaluation.[2] It remains to advance – if not to complete, in a single collection of essays focused on such issues as they arise in certain forms of personal narrative – this act of scholarly acknowledgment.

'The point on which the author failed to please himself,' wrote Henry Adams in the preface he prepared for the signature of Henry Cabot Lodge and placed before his 'own' preface in the 1918 edition of the *Education*, '. . . was the usual one of literary form.' In terms of literary-historical chronology, this study commences in its first two chapters with considerations of two works of

1907 (Adams circulated the *Education* privately in that year and Henry James published *The American Scene*) in which the authors develop solutions to the problems of literary form posed by their perceptions of their material. Each book is in a sense an effort to revise the relation between inner and outer realities, to reinterpret a changed America in the light of re-examined personal outlook. Each writer is, and is not, generally 'pleased' by the result — Adams strategically feigns dissatisfaction, while James's aesthetic confidence overlies unresolved anxieties. But each also arrives at an *un*usual answer to a no-longer-'usual' question of narrative procedure, centered in self-portrayal as author-protagonist in a mixed, improvisatory form of personal narrative. The experience, however, of the two other major members of the literary generation of Adams and James — William Dean Howells and Samuel Clemens — may be briefly introduced in prefatory refinement of the issues to be pursued in the chapters to follow. At stages of life and career similar to those at which Adams and James produced the books in question, Howells and Clemens also felt a sense of broken relation with the culture of which they were in many ways representative, a need to reinvent a narrative bond between personal upheaval within and accelerating change in America without.

During the 1880s a complex combination of private and public pressures profoundly affected Howells's priorities as a novelist, and he was dominated at the end of the decade by the urge to represent in fiction his personal consciousness of social crisis in America. In *A Hazard of New Fortunes* (1890) he attempted to produce a novel that would combine multiple plots and a panoramic range of characters with a near-autobiographical record of his move from Boston to New York, and within this emblematic 'journey' to explore his own response to the new actualities of urban America. The novel communicates a painfully direct sense of Howells's only partially successful effort to relate a traumatically altered personal outlook to sweeping, even violent, historical change. But it also marks the beginning of his loss of novelistic power, notwithstanding that he wrote many novels thereafter and continued to exert his authority as a man of letters. *A Hazard* fails to integrate his intensified autobiographical response to social and economic shifts, and fails structurally to cohere. Committed to the novel as a form, he did not on the other hand develop a documentary mode capable of taking the imprint of his artist's imagination of the rifts he saw widening in American society, through fissures in his sense of the continuity of his personal existence. *A Hazard* shows him reaching, however, toward a mixed narrative form in which to explore and express the relation between personal and cultural exigency.

Clemens, too, found as the century expired that the already accomplished art of his fiction, the 'completed' image (however filled with unresolved private and public tension) of himself as American writer, was inadequate to his own sense of onrushing change without and of erupting disturbance within. The release of Mark Twain's fictive imagination through early autobiographical exploration of his experience on the frontier and along the Mississippi is well documented. But his eventual loss of fictionalizing power − the progressive overwhelming of his later stories by his own polemical voice − remains on the whole less satisfactorily accounted for in terms of neurosis, personal misfortune or the inevitable inroads of age. The violently fragmented state of his latest narratives, straining against their own denials of coherence in history, society or self, seems in retrospect, in the context of this study, less purely a matter of waning imaginative force. It seems more a matter of an active, furious if futile, search for alternative literary form, through which to express a predominating sense of disconnection from a disintegrating universe, personal and familial in one dimension, cosmic in another, but American in a way that encompasses both. The posthumous *Autobiography* in its published versions, and the centrifugal mass of autobiographical dictations which still defy definitive publication, are in this light, however failed and formless, the ultimate and inevitable mode of Clemens's self-narration. He observes at one point, as an obstacle to autobiographical narrative, that 'life does not consist mainly − or even largely − of facts or happenings. It consists mainly of the storm of thoughts,'[3] unsubduable in usual autobiographical terms, or for Clemens in any others that he can devise. The storm of thought, swirling through his late obsession with personal narrative, makes insoluble for Clemens the problem of literary form, the problem in fact for Adams as well as Clemens of form in both history and personality, and therefore in autobiographical art.

The case of Clemens thus contains an emblem of autobiographical impasse, with serious consequences for his survival as an artist in his previously accustomed narrative mode. This in no way need reflect adversely on his overall achievement, or on the value of all his accumulated writing as a kind of personal record − God's Fool had been from the very beginning part and parcel of the Wild Humorist of the Pacific Slope. But his failure to solve, in sustained and stable narrative, the twin crises of personal and cultural coherence experienced by Howells but absorbed and reprojected more successfully by Adams and James in the *Education* and *The American Scene*, provides an inverse point of reference for discussion of the works on which these chapters focus. Each, in some way, constitutes an act of narrative passage through some such potential or actual impasse, the personal and the literary survival of such crisis interlinked. In each, in some fashion, what Adams called the usual problem of literary form is engaged through resolution in the self, as protagonist in personal narrative, of contending reportorial, fictional, historiographical or traditionally autobiographical objectives and resources.

In the process the usual problem of procedure is itself transformed into a literary-technical situation for the author which invariably − however variously for different writers − becomes a 'central and not peripheral' aspect (to borrow Cox's phrase used in reference to American autobiographical tradition) of the protagonist's situation in relation to his subject. The problem of form remains 'usual' in the sense of necessary, inescapable, perhaps even to some degree insoluble or soluble only for the narrative moment. But it is hardly in these works the traditionally known quantity which Adams (knowing by then the *extra*ordinary nature of narrative in the *Education*) termed it in all seeming innocence in 'Lodge's' preface. As with Clemens, disturbance rather than serenity of sensibility, in response to instabilities within and without, is the source of narrative energy. As also with Clemens, but to more decisive and successfully innovative formal effect, a persona's sense of shifting yet continuous relation between personal and compositional predicament is an element of that impetus, the intensities of the storm of thought negotiated rather than circumnavigated in narrative.

In his recent essay called 'Autobiography and the Cultural Moment,' James Olney seems at once to continue in the light of subsequent studies the line of inquiry contained in Cox's 'Autobiography and America,' and to reassert as still central to the issue Cox's concern with the need for terms. If anything, Olney's sense of that need is more acute, just as autobiography remains for him 'the most elusive of literary documents':

One never knows where or how to take hold of autobiography: there are simply no general rules available . . . . In talking about autobiography, one always feels that there is a great and present danger that the subject will slip away altogether, . . . that there is no way to bring autobiography to heel as a literary genre with its own proper form, terminology, and observances. On the other hand, . . . there arises the opposite temptation . . . to argue not only that autobiography exists but that it *alone* exists — that all writing that aspires to be literature is autobiography and nothing else.[4]

This book means neither to bring a genre 'to heel' nor to argue its omnipresence (still less therefore to be itself principally a work of personal narrative, except in the sense that all readers become the chroniclers, if not always in writing, of the personal experience of a text). This book does, however, seek to develop terms applicable to a range of twentieth-century American personal narratives, and to locate the American autobiographical impulse in a range of works resistant to the traditional observances of *any* genre, let alone those of autobiography. Hence a tendency in the following chapters to prefer the adjectival to the nominal — autobiographi*cal* to autobiograph*y* — and beyond that a tendency to prefer 'personal narrative' as more flexibly and accurately accommodating the features of the books and the strategies or instincts of the writers considered. Sharing Olney's sense of the theoretical elusiveness of such literary documents, I also, and for reasons principally inherent in the documents themselves, prefer to press toward closer definition of the ways in which — in the individual case — multiple literary means and ends are invested in, enacted through, and thus in the end transmuted into, the autobiographical. This while such works also do, or this as a necessary means toward doing, some form of justice to their other, less personal subjects.

This book is therefore conceived as progressively unified from within a sequence of separate analyses. Its chapters are meant to be, as James Agee said of the relation between his text and Walker Evans's photographs in *Let Us Now Praise Famous Men*, 'mutually independent and fully collaborative.' Collaboration in the case of this study, however, is intended to overtake, without obscuring, the independence of the several sections, through accumulating systems of cross-reference among them. These are systems of *self*-interrelation and association among modern American author-protagonists, whatever their awareness or unawarenesses of one another, as much as they are the impositions of analysis. They constitute the 'net,' as James put it in his own persona as *The American Scene*'s 'restless analyst,' cast over 'interlinked appearances' from within a mind in the process of unifying its own experience.

Additional books, by other writers, could of course have been represented: Stein's *The Autobiography of Alice B. Toklas* or Conrad Aiken's *Ushant*, for example, to name two well-known third-personal narratives; the case of Nabokov's *Speak, Memory*, a novelist's autobiographical 'revisitation' of the no-longer-fully *Conclusive Evidence* of his life in art; much of the writing, whatever the form in which presented, of Henry Miller or Anaïs Nin; Dos Passos's effort to contain a nation's consciousness in *U.S.A.*; the essays of Edward Hoagland, in whose attention to the natural world is fused a full consciousness of post-Adams cosmos and culture with an evident awareness of the preceptorship of Henry David Thoreau. On the range of works finally included, however – from Adams and James through Mailer and Joan Didion – and on their confluence of American sensibility, this inquiry into these issues must now stand.

Such narrative confluence of American lives has been from the outset the making, as well as grounds for the understanding, of much of American literary culture. Whatever the ways in which the modern works studied here view the outward America through the inward American eye, and 'I,' an encounter with an idea of America's past and future condensed into the personal present, a sense of autobiographical encounter with the cultural moment, is common to them all. In a strict literary sense as well as in a broader one, and in Gertrude Stein's phrase, in the making by these writers – standing here for many more – of their chapters of experience is the making of Americans.

Acknowledgments

I am grateful to all my colleagues within the University of Tulsa's Graduate Faculty of Modern Letters (now part of the Faculty of English Language and Literature), for their support and knowledgable interest in the development of this book. Thomas F. Staley has in particular been unfailingly encouraging, and he along with Winston Weathers and Darcy O'Brien read and made useful comments on portions of the manuscript.

Richard Poirier has also given time and valuable advice in connection with several chapters and with the inquiry's general concerns.

Many people in addition have at one time or another given me the benefit of their insight concerning various aspects of this study, among them Daniel Aaron, Warner Berthoff, Michael G. Cooke, F. W. Dupee, Warren French, Arnold Goldman, Norman S. Grabo, James D. Hart, Richard Hutson, U. C. Knoepflmacher, Josephine Miles, Felicity Nussbaum, Joel Porte, John Henry Raleigh, Henry Nash Smith, Helen Vendler, Kingsley Widmer and Larzer Ziff. Richard Bridgman, at a certain juncture, alerted me to relevant materials and asked questions about the book's emerging outlines, my reflection on which can only have improved the result. Any errors of judgment or fact remain my own.

I wish also to thank my graduate students, particularly those in my course on autobiography in American literature, but those too with whom I have talked, in or out of class, in Tulsa and elsewhere, about a broad range of issues bearing on this subject. Association with them continues to be one of the profession's chief rewards.

Thanks are also due, for a summer Faculty Research Fellowship granted toward completion of the manuscript, to the University of Tulsa's Office of Research and to the members of the selection committee.

Portions of this book have appeared previously, in slightly or substantially different form, in *American Literature, Genre, The Georgia Review* and the *Journal of American Studies*. For permission to publish from this material I am grateful to the editors of those journals. Alfred A. Knopf, Inc., Faber and Faber Limited, Farrar, Straus & Giroux, Inc., Harcourt Brace Jovanovich, Inc., Houghton Mipplin Company, Little, Brown and Company, Random House, Inc., and Simon & Schuster have kindly granted permission to reprint material under copyright.

T. M. Farmiloe, of The Macmillan Press Ltd, has my sincere appreciation for his interest in the project, as does Julia Steward for her editorial wisdom and concern throughout production. I appreciate as well the efforts of those involved in St. Martin's Press's co-publication in America.

I am, as always, irredeemably in the debt of my wife, Tatiana Marinovich Taylor.

Tulsa, Oklahoma   GORDON O. TAYLOR

1

Of Adams and Aquarius: Henry Adams and Norman Mailer

Here was a breach of continuity — a rupture in historical sequence! Was it real, or only apparent? One's personal universe hung on the answer . . .

The Education of Henry Adams

No, the difficulty is that the history is interior . . .

The Armies of the Night

Lodged at the Hay-Adams in Washington on the eve of the 1967 March on the Pentagon, Norman Mailer muses in the third person in *The Armies of the Night* on his hostelry's namesakes and the relation between their world and his own: 'One may wonder if the Adams in the name of his hotel bore any relation to Henry; we need not be concerned with Hay who was a memorable and accomplished gentleman from the nineteenth century . . . .'[1] The Adams was indeed Henry (as Mailer surely knew), but more interesting is Mailer's separation of Adams from his appropriation of John Hay as representative of 'a time when men and events were solid, comprehensible, often obedient to a code of values, and resolutely nonelectronic,' a time Mailer thus sets in opposition to his own. Adams fades from the passage, yet one may continue to wonder about him; whereas the passage proceeds to deal with Hay, with whom we need not be concerned precisely because he is dismissable (by Mailer) as a nineteenth-century gentleman.

What might one have gone on to say about Adams, himself a

1

memorable nineteenth-century gentleman whatever else he more importantly was in the history of American ideas? Might one have wondered if it could be said at all of Adams, as it is confidently said here of Hay, that he was 'from the nineteenth century'? Drifting, disembodied intelligence that he imagined himself at last, Adams insisted he was 'from' the eighteenth century, or even the twelfth, when not brooding across infinitely broader vistas of evolutionary or geological time: the nineteenth century finally for him a rift in the cultural formation rather than the bedrock of personal experience. But it is the 'man-meteorite' of the late chapters of the *Education*, accelerating through fields of twentieth-century force, whose path on the periphery of Mailer's thought disturbs for a moment his paradigm of nineteenth-century coherence. Conjured or not, the shade of Henry Adams as prophetic twentieth-century sensibility impinges here on Mailer's sense of literary purpose.

Slender grounds for an assertion of relationship between Adams and Mailer; as well, to be sure, a familiar notion, that the *Education* has much to suggest as to the *in*substantiality, *in*comprehensibility, *dis*obedience to supposed values, even the electronic excitation, of twentieth-century men and events. Yet the sense of Adams as a spectral presider over certain of Mailer's recent efforts — to plot the directions and gauge the velocities of the age by registering the impact of a defining event on his imagination — is recurrent and at times pervasive in *Of a Fire on the Moon*. Indeed this book occasionally invites as subtitle 'The Education of Aquarius,' the name Mailer adopts for his third-personal narrative just as Adams portrays an 'Adams' as much protagonist as persona.

Both books are concerned (as Alfred Kazin says of the *Education* alone) with 'history . . . recast as individual experience and speculation';[2] both writers project themselves as author-protagonists intent on absorbing and reacting to a set of facts, a sequence of events, a body of ideas. Personal consciousness of history, imaginative embodiment of facts, events, ideas, is at once the theme and the representational aim of each. The issue is one neither of direct influence nor of precise symmetries between the *Education* (1918) and *Of a Fire* (1970), the one so private in initial conception and circulation (in 1907) yet clearly expectant of public attention, the other first commissioned by *Life* and thus utterly public yet clearly of private importance to its author. It is rather a question of tonal and strategic affinities, of convergences in the self-characterizations of Adams and Aquarius.

Adams concludes the *Education* with the report of Hay's death in 1905, presenting it as a portent of his own, and subsuming in Hay's loss the death of Clarence King and the assassinations of Lincoln, Garfield and McKinley. Nineteenth-century America itself, mortally wounded by civil war, seems to have lingered forty more years and expired at last along with Hay, the new century having been prematurely born and gathering force all the while. (Adams had already seen the forces of the future in the dynamos of the Chicago and Paris Expositions.) While Adams's sense of expended, 'posthumous' calm finds fullest expression here in his closing pages, it is a premise of his attitude toward himself and his time from the outset, the condition out of which the entire narrative proceeds.

Mailer begins *Of a Fire on the Moon* by establishing his perspective as Aquarius through a comparable use of his response to Ernest Hemingway's suicide in 1961. 'Wedded to horror' and thoughts of death ever since — though his early sense of literary lineage from Hemingway had long since developed into a broader spectrum of relations with previous American writers — Mailer subsumes in this loss the assassinations of the Kennedys, of Malcolm X and Martin Luther King, the flames of the ghettos and of Vietnam. The whole decade of the 1960s, of disintegrative conflict approaching civil war, is seen as prefigured in the Hemingway shotgun blast. If Mailer's 1960s, an accelerated form of the 1860s and thereafter for Adams, were the throes of one century already being supplanted by another, they were also in Mailer's view — as the decade of a venture calling not simply for a new technology but requiring in consequence a new man — the historical hinge on which the twenty-first century would prematurely hinge.

Mailer's mood in 1969, like Adams's in 1905, is spent, detached. The exhaustions of the decade have left him feeling like 'some just-consumed essence of the past,' a 'disembodied' condition he finds appropriate to his literary task in terms reminiscent of Adams's strategic self-effacement:

> He has learned to live with questions. Of course, as always, he has little to do with the immediate spirit of the time, . . . he has never had less sense of possessing the age. He feels in fact little more than a decent spirit, somewhat shunted to the side. It is the best possible position for detective work.[3]

The questions with which Aquarius is now to live are quite different from those inhabiting Adams's mind. Mailer's periodic need to ask, for example, despite his inability to know, whether the best or the worst of the age's energies have lifted men to the moon and toward the stars, bears little direct relation to Adam's recurrent need to ponder, despite his inability to accept, a moral equivalent to evolutionary law or a law of historical acceleration. Yet as metaphysical deeps, surrounding like water a diving mind and absorbing all traces of its passage, such questions become for both writers the encompassing medium, rather than the immediate objects, of their powers of literary detection. Thus for Mailer, hours before launching of the moonship, 'like a dive into a dream, explorations of these questions would only open into deeper questions. Standing in the early morning heat, he had an instinct that before all was done the questions would travel through the unmapped continent of America's undetermined heart.' 'Before all was done' indeed; for in each book the main lines of imaginative and rhetorical force are lines of questioning less able to 'do' than to sense and sift out 'all' they might entail, less intent on answers than on images embodying the mind's 'travel' toward answers.

Both men are more immediately concerned to detect psychological clues to historical or philosophical mysteries. Of all Adams's studies, 'the one he would rather have avoided was that of his own mind.' Nevertheless, that is precisely the method of the *Education*, as well as his avenue of approach to other studies: 'the universe could be known only as motion of mind . . . . One could know it only as one's self.' Mailer, like Adams a writer whose assertions of 'loss of ego' fail to convince even as they perform successfully other rhetorical tasks, has also constructed a situation requiring constant self-scrutiny even as it posits a protagonist able to 'let his ego float off to whatever would receive it.' If Mailer's ostensible models for a psychology of the year 2000 are the Apollo astronauts, whereas Adams is thrown back wholly on himself in trying to fix a psychology of 1900, Aquarius is nonetheless absorbed in the problem of his own relation to these 'new men.' They seem to him 'as far away as history' behind quarantine glass at a prelaunch press conference. Yet he gauges proximity as well as distance while thinking that 'one would have nothing to measure them by until the lines of the new psychology had begun to be drawn':

Yes, Aquarius thought, astronauts have learned not only to live with opposites, but it was conceivable that the contradictions in their nature were so located in the very impetus of the age that their personality might begin to speak, for better or worse, of some new psychological constitution to man . . . . On the one hand to dwell in the very center of technological reality . . . yet to inhabit − if only in one's dreams − that other world where . . . the unanswerable questions of eternity must reside, was to suggest natures so divided that they could have been the most miserable and unbalanced of men if they did not contain in their huge contradictions some of the profound and accelerating opposites of the century itself.[4]

Adams too had felt himself at an impassable distance from the 'new American' of 1900, as if viewing him through a glass barrier between centuries, but had been 'beyond measure curious' about his own relation to this 'child born of contact between the new and the old energies.' On the one hand

he could see that the new American − the child of incalculable coal-power, chemical power, electric power, and radiating energy, as well as of new forces yet undetermined − must be a sort of God compared with any former creation of nature. At the rate of progress since 1800, every American who lived into the year 2000 would know how to control unlimited power. He would think in complexities unimaginable to an earlier mind.[5]

Poor prophecy, even granting an undercurrent of skepticism, but interesting in view of Mailer's preoccupation with the question of a god-like as against an ignoble and demented drive toward the moon. Interesting too in view of Adams's suggestion earlier that these unimaginable complexities of mind would be rooted in the fact that 'mathematics had become the only necessary language of thought' in 1900. This notion is basic to Mailer's 'psychology of astronauts,' emphasizing incorporation of human thought and speech into the circuitry and vocabulary of the computer.

Yet there is on the other hand in Adams's effort to grasp the nature of an emerging mind a note of greater personal involvement in a process less clearly foreseen. Adams along with the new American 'would need to think in contradictions'; Adams too faces the 'violently coercive' realignment of mind by 'the next great

influx of forces.' 'Prolonged one generation longer' (beyond 1900
– Adams would die in 1918 and Mailer be born in 1923), this
process 'would require a new social mind. As though thought were
common salt in indefinite solution it must enter a new phase
subject to new laws. Thus far, since five or ten thousand years, the
mind had successfully reacted, and nothing yet proved that it
would fail to react – but it would need to jump.' Images of himself
as a meteoroid, as 'falling forever in space,' as Adams struggles to
render the sensation of approach to this crisis – or of Americans
'drifting unconsciously to some point in thought, as their solar
system was said to be drifting towards some point in space' – find
echoes in Mailer's imagery suggesting a 'jump' in consciousness
toward some interface in intelligence. Aquarius too feels 'his mind
indeed out in some weightless trip through the vacuum of a psychic
space,' drawn like Adams's toward metamorphosis by gathering
technological force.

If the technologies in question are different – Adams's dynamo
as against Mailer's rocket, looking like a 'white stone Madonna' as
if in reference to a less comforting Virgin than Adams had
imagined, now reunited with the dynamo in a new and more
ominous Chartres – the responses they provoke are similar.
Thematic emphasis is in each case on evolutionary transformation; the metaphorical thrust, however, is for both toward
annihilation. Thus for Adams, 'the mind had already entered a
field of attraction so violent that it must immediately pass beyond,
into new equilibrium . . . to suffer dissipation altogether.'
Aquarius prepares in imagination to go with the astronauts
'through the funnel of a historical event whose significance might
yet be next to death itself.' (Yet he adds, 'Was it like that as one was
waiting to be born?' The tensed expectancy of some rough birth in
the turning of a technological gyre occurs now and then in the tone
of both books.) Neither can see with certainty beyond the funnel of
the twentieth century, the one having felt himself pulled into it as
early as 1870, the other feeling himself spun out of it as early as
1970. (Let us, like both writers throughout their volumes, 'take
mild pleasure in conjunction of dates,' as Mailer puts it.) But the
century remains for Mailer – his 'ship of flames' having surged
into space, its 'metaphysical direction unknown' – what it became
for Adams, 'a century which moved with the most magnificent display of power into directions it could not comprehend.'

At the outset of *Mont-Saint-Michel and Chartres*, Adams calls the Abbey on the Mount 'the starting point of all our future travels. Here is your first eleventh-century church! How does it affect you?' In *Of a Fire on the Moon*, Mailer takes as an architectural starting point for a 'philosophical launch' toward the future a building he calls 'the first cathedral of the age of technology,' the huge Vehicle Assembly Building at Cape Kennedy. Surrounded by a history of its own in obsolete towers standing as 'monoliths and artifacts of a prehistoric period' in rocketry, it affects Aquarius in contrasting ways. From without he finds it ugly, its decoration in 'concentric rectangles of green-gray and charcoal-gray, ivory-gray and light blue-gray' a plasticized parody of the smoky outer surfaces of old stained glass. 'Once inside, however, it was conceivably one of the more beautiful buildings of the world,' and his description of the interior gleams in Adamsian response ('A pure medievalist is Aquarius!') to the juncture in this place of new forces and forms:

> the light which filtered through translucent panels rising from floor to ceiling was dim, hardly brighter than the light in a church or an old railroad terminal. One lost in consequence any familiar sense of recognition . . . you could have been standing on the scaffolding of an unfinished but monumental cathedral, beautiful in this dim light, this smoky concatenation of structure upon structure, of breadths and vertigos and volumes of open space beneath the ceiling, tantalizing views of immense rockets hidden by their clusters of work platforms.[6]

'The great churches of a religious age,' among which Mailer lists 'Mont-Saint Michel, Chartres,' have become 'this warehouse of the gods,' vacuously named but undeniably felt as the locus of power. Adams had seen in the resolved quality of Gothic line, its finished effect even in ruin, the last unity of aspiration with knowledge in the Western mind. The unfinished, multi-structured character of this building reflects for Aquarius the indecipherable relation between aspirations and techniques gestating within:

> but he was standing at least in the first cathedral of the age of technology, and he might as well recognize that the world would change, that the world *had* changed . . . . And it had changed in ways he did not recognize, had never anticipated, and could possibly not comprehend now. The change was mightier than

he had counted on. The full brawn of the rocket came over him in this cavernous womb of an immensity, this giant cathedral of a machine designed to put together another machine which would voyage through space. Yes, this emergence of a ship to travel the ether was no event he could measure by any philosophy he had been able to put together in his brain.[7]

There is something here, and in the previous passage, of Adams's 'religious' reaction to the dynamo at Paris in 1900:

> As he grew accustomed to the great gallery of machines, he began to feel the forty-foot dynamos as a moral force, much as the early Christians felt the Cross. The planet itself seemed less impressive, in its old-fashioned, deliberate, annual or daily revolution, than this huge wheel, revolving within arm's length at some vertiginous speed, and barely murmuring – scarcely humming an audible warning to stand a hair's-breadth further for respect of power – while it would not wake the baby lying close against its frame. Before the end, one began to pray to it; inherited instinct taught the natural expression of man before silent and infinite force. Among the thousand symbols of ultimate energy, the dynamo was not so human as some, but it was the most expressive.[8]

Mailer's eschatological interest – 'Man was voyaging to the planets in order to look for God. Or was it to destroy Him?' – likewise springs from direct response rather than abstract theme. As the ship ascends, impossibly silent until cataracts of sound to match those of fire overwhelm the observer, it occurs to Aquarius 'that man now had something with which to speak to God.' Adams's thought, in the passage just quoted, then turns from the dynamo to 'the new rays,' and he too feels himself (in Mailer's phrase and like Mailer in the VAB) in 'the antechamber of a new Creation' without instruments of philosophical measure: 'In these seven years [since 1893 when Roentgen discovered X-rays] man had translated himself into a new universe which had no common scale of measurement with the old.'

One scale of measurement briefly considered by both authors is that of the dream. The psychology of astronauts commences for Aquarius in a recurring dream Neil Armstrong reportedly had as a boy, in which he would hold his breath and hover in air. Unconcerned to verify this, Mailer 'chooses to believe' it as '*fact*' (italics his), as if thus more purely to possess in imagination an emblem from 'the inner space' of a journey to the outer. Such an emblem may then be charged, not only with personal dreads inadmissable to consciousness, but also with some sense of the cultural dangers of a leap into the void. Perhaps the 'voyage to the moon was finally an exploration by the century itself into the possible consequences of its worship of technology.' These too are considerations denied on the technological surface of an event nevertheless a 'mystery beneath.' Mailer thus establishes a reference point in the topography of unconscious life, on a corrective order of magnitude in which the convolutions of the dream — nebulae of metaphysical stuff — fuse with the camera-recorded sight of 'real' nebulae floating in space immeasurably far beyond.

Adams's insights into unconscious life are fragmentary and dispersed, but their argumentative and metaphorical functions are comparable to those of Aquarius's commitment to the '*fact*' of a prophetic dream. For Adams too the nebulous configurations of inner being are the fundamental fact of psychic life. He too is less concerned to verify their existence than to build some image of their energies into the record of his waking thought. His speculations on the nature of historical process, and the impact of new physics on old metaphysics, are thus also provided with a corrective reference point, an interior landmark from which he commences his ventures into exterior phenomena, and to which he always returns: 'The only absolute truth was the subconscious chaos below.' Adams's mind, its normalcy redefined as 'dispersion, sleep, dream,' becomes an image mediating among equally unstable conditions on other orders of magnitude. The microcosmic abyss of subatomic particles, the macrocosmic gulf of the stellar universe — a historical formula has somehow in Adams's view to meet the objective conditions of both. Yet conditions within the atom, or the galaxy, are of interest, indeed are 'real,' only as they help him express the subjective reality, the '*fact*' at this point in history of his own consciousness-as-dream.

Another scale of measurement lies in the work of other artists in other art forms. Like Adams a self-described 'amateur of the mysteries of form,' Mailer invokes Cézanne: 'Something in that vision spoke like the voice of the century to come . . . . Art had embarked on an entrance into the long tunnel where aesthetics met technology.' Cézanne, whose paintings were shown at the Paris Exposition, was among those to whom Adams was unable to respond. But if Adams 'did not know how to look at the art exhibits of 1900,' Mailer is uncertain how to look at those of 1970, in which 'the artist had crossed from the brush to the wind machine and blew up walls of plastic through which the patron all blindfolded would creep.' In Paris as in Chicago in 1893, Adams 'lingered long among the dynamos,' as if they in their huge galleries were the art works of the new age. Mailer would later find that 'the art of communication had become the mechanical function, and the machine was the work of art.'

At Parisian exhibits of 1892, Adams had been

> racked by the effort of art to be original, and when one day, after much reflection, John La Farge asked whether there might not still be room for something simple in art, Adams shook his head. As he saw the world, it was no longer simple and could not express itself simply. It should express what it was; and that was something that neither Adams nor La Farge understood.
>
> Under the first blast of this furnace-heat, the lights seemed fairly to go out. He felt nothing in common with the world as it promised to be.[9]

Confronted with a painting by René Magritte, Aquarius feels similarly perplexed, in a moment of similarly dimmed narrative lighting on all but the picture itself,

> a startling image of a room with an immense rock situated in the center of the floor. The instant of time suggested by the canvas was comparable to the mood of a landscape in the instant just before something awful is about to happen, or just after, one could not tell . . . . [I]t was as if Magritte had listened to the ending of one world with its comfortable chairs in the parlor, and heard the intrusion of a new world, silent as the windowless stone which grew in the room . . . . Now the world of the future was a dead rock, and the rock was in the room.[10]

In so far as Mailer attaches this image specifically to the moon-flight, its portent for the spiritual consequences of a worship of technology is clear: 'The silences of the canvas spoke' of dead men in dead spacecraft; 'the painting could have been photographed for the front page [Mailer chose it for the dust jacket] − it hung from the wall like a severed head.' The Magritte is Mailer's nearest approach to answering his unanswerable question, a question in other contexts also Adams's: what 'revelation of the real intent of History' might the hieroglyphic of the event contain?

Yet the passage's symbolic energy really flows the other way, arrested short of completed interpretation. Emphasis here, and in general throughout both books, is on the moment of imaginative crisis, the instant of time enfolding some shift in the nature of reality as perceived or experienced. Imagination at the edge of change — drawn toward an act of prophetic judgment which might carry it intact across a fracture in time or in the continuity of intelligence — rather than imagination in the conclusive prophetic act: this is the basic stuff of both narratives, the self-characterizing force in both Adams and Aquarius. As for Adams's contemplation of the Saint-Gaudens sculpture at the grave of his wife, whose suicide heightened his sense of life 'cut in halves' by historical tendencies, so for each author's efforts to envision symbolically the rupture of one world by intrusion of another, be the image dynamo or rocket, *Pteraspis* fossil or a rock in a room: 'The interest of the figure was not in its meaning, but in the response of the observer.'

Adams and Aquarius have other interests in common, their perspectives taken from opposite ends of the century's 'funnel,' their observer's responses suggesting more similarity than difference between these vantage points as imaginative states. Both sense a 'strangeness' enforced on them by the accelerating pace of American events. Adams, returning from England in 1868, 'could hardly have been stranger on the shore of a world, so changed from what it had been ten years before,' had he been debarking from a Tyrian Galley of 1000 BC. Mailer, confronting in 1969 a world markedly changed from what it had been for him ten years before, is 'like a stranger. He feels in such surroundings a foreigner equally as much as he feels American.' Both allude to Matthew Arnold while evoking this atmosphere of estrangement. For Adams, the 'process that . . . Arnold described as wandering between two worlds, one dead, the other powerless to be born, helps nothing' in his effort to fix his own position. Yet whatever the lines in 'Stanzas from the Grande Chartreuse' lack in the help Adams is seeking — a new world in his view already powerfully born — they inform our sense of past and future contained in the precarious present moment of his imagination. Mailer attributes the astronauts' demeanor to the 'complacent assumption that the universe was no majestic mansion of architectonics out there between evil and nobility, or strife on a darkling plain, but rather an ultimately benign field of investigation.' His reference to 'Dover Beach' is fleeting, but even if only an imaginative reflex it is to a poem which is similar in its focus on the personal sense of historical crisis to that quoted by Adams. *'Fin de siècle'* is for Mailer a 'September' mood, described half in terms of a historian's instinct that 'the century was done' in 1969, half in terms of a personal 'burial by sea' of the years of a failing marriage. For Adams 'November' is the month, more mental than calendrical, conveying his sense of *fin de siècle*, a comparable combination of historical verdict and personal grief.

The moments at which Adams and Aquarius seem most closely attuned, however, are those in which they contemplate — as general backdrop to particular subjects, with mutual awe underlying disparate interests — the architectonics of the universe. For Adams the last embodiment of such principles and processes in a majestic structure evenly situated between evil and nobility was the cathedral at Chartres. There, and nowhere since, all balances were struck, all lines of aspiration and inertia resolved, all orders of magnitude symbolically accommodated. Now, for both Mailer and Adams, it is the unresolved process, the ongoing, unfinishable structuring of the mansion out there among unfixable loci, that fascinates. Both are drawn to wonder at, as exhaustless sources of metaphor — as often as they are forced to acknowledge, as obstacles to complete explanation — the mystery and magic at the heart of science. The inexplicability of gravity, magnetism, electricity, despite the weight of technique resting on man's awareness of their presence as forces; the proliferation in 1969 as in 1900 of subatomic particles discernible to man; the subtle betrayals constantly occurring on the border between theory and application; these are only some of the mystifications affecting Adams's search for historical formulae, or Mailer's for the meaning of man's venture into space. Energy is the primal mystery, and there for both writers the ultimate problems insolubly reside:

> If there is a crossing in the intellectual cosmos where philosophical notions of God, man, and the machine can come together it is probably to be found in the conceptual swamps which surround every notion of energy. The greatest mystery in the unremitting mysteries of physics must be the nature of energy itself — is it the currency of the universe or the agent of

creation? The basic stuff of life or merely the fuel of life? The guard of the heavens, or the heart and blood of time? The mightiest gates of the metaphysician hinge on the incomprehensibility yet human intimacy of that ability to perform work and initiate movement which rides through the activities of men and machines, and powers the cycles of nature.[11]

The words are Mailer's, but Adams says (rather asks) as much. The dynamo spins at such a crossing in Adams's intellectual cosmos, but its capacity for generating symbolic power depends on rather than dispels the mystery: 'he could see only an absolute *fiat* in electricity as in faith.' According to Aquarius, the savage mind 'looked once at fire and knew' its source. We, however, have long forgotten, and so like Adams have become wandering 'pilgrims of power' even as we launch ships presuming to control the forces of fire and thought — essences of prehistoric ritual — through rockets and computers.

The laws of thermodynamics provide Adams with partial fulfillment of his pilgrimage, a means of harnessing as historical force within an intellectual scheme physical energies which are ultimately mysterious and intellectually inaccessible. A dynamic theory of history and a law of acceleration thus emerge for him from the abyss of ignorance (these phrases appearing as titles to late chapters of the *Education*). So in the physics of rocketry Mailer finds theoretical bases from which to launch conjectures as to the historical design within the technological act, itself precariously predicated on the mysteries of energy. A cautious 'preference' for the notion of deep-running purpose in space flight, a hope at the least of new prospect on 'the Lord and the Lucifer' within man himself, emerges from Mailer's conjectural probes. We need not be surprised, however, if such answers seem weak, curiously void of the forces on which they are based, and which are vividly felt as the questions themselves are engaged. Adams's thermodynamics, after all, like Mailer's interest in propulsion and trajectory as analogues to the thrusts and arcings of human thought, is a system of metaphor dependent for imaginative life on the very mysteries it is aimed at solving.

It is as questions posed anew, enriched rather than unraveled by the responsive inquirer, that the 'answers' these books afford retain interest and energy. And indeed the voices of Adams and Aquarius shift back to the interrogative before falling into final cadences, fatigued yet clarified, of personal valediction. Adams asks, in the language of experiment, whether the mind will this time survive the 'jump' into its inevitable new phase. Aquarius asks of an actual moon sample, sealed in glass and thus seeming as likely to have dropped from Magritte's painting as to have been quarried in space, 'Marvellous little moon rock. What the Devil did it say?' As a seeker after quantitative solutions, whose announcements of such solutions betray his need to explore beyond them, Adams — in the Parisian summer of his final paragraphs, in the silent 'void' of his life's broken orbit — seems once more to converge with Aquarius's summation:

> Yes, he had come to believe by the end of this long summer that probably we had to explore into outer space, for technology had penetrated the modern mind to such a depth that . . . we might have to go out into space until the mystery of new discovery would force us to regard the world once again as poets, behold it as savages who knew that if the universe was a lock, its key was metaphor rather than measure.[12]

Attempting to break from historical gravity through his Polynesian travels, Adams had felt much the same. And the *Education* explores the space of his awareness to similar concluding effect.

Having begun with and returned to the notion of convergence in self-characterization, we may consider the idea of 'convergence' itself. In its mathematical sense it has a certain application to the discussion, for it is precisely when 'approaching a limit' in the author-protagonist's ability to absorb and comprehend the near-present as history that the narrative lines approach intersection. Aquarius calls it 'his profession [as "novelist" in a sense subsuming the historian, the reporter, the autobiographer] to live alone with thoughts at the very edge of his mental reach.' By this definition, Adams in the *Education* is a novelist as well, in a sense subsuming as many literary roles. It matters little whether one 'echoes' or 'anticipates' the other; the interest is all in resemblances between their efforts to bring their responses under literary control.

In its biological sense — as 'adaptive evolution of superficially similar structures in unrelated species subjected to similar environments' — convergence suggests other possibilities. Mailer and Adams face in these volumes predicaments of understanding and expression constituting similar imaginative environments. Adams's exposition, for example, of the sensations of metaphysical un-control, of the 'surge of a supersensual chaos' sweeping over the nineteenth century's religio-scientific landmarks like 'the green water of the deep-sea ocean,' is analogous to Mailer's soundings of the 'bottomless,' 'underwater' sensations occasioned by the twentieth century's loss or multiplicity of philosophical bearings. Both sequences reveal something of the discontinuity between what was known and what now needs to be known, or between what was unknowable (but could therefore be kept at a safe mental distance) and what is now known (but can therefore no longer be avoided). Something is correspondingly revealed of the demands placed by such discontinuities on the writer's skill as literary engineer, if not to bridge the gulf at least to construct an observation platform extending beyond the brink.

One may then theorize an evolutionary link between the author-protagonists of the *Education* and *Of a Fire on the Moon*, residing in both the common aspects of their imaginative situations and the similar structures of their responses to those situations. Many of these structures of response are more than superficially similar, however unrelated in other ways the literary 'species' of Adams and Mailer remain. If Adams's questionings come to rest in 'Hamlet's Shakespearean silence,' there is in such silence and appropriation of a name a link in self-characterization with Mailer's own pre-sumption to Lear-like rage in the face of insoluble dilemmas: 'Rave on, he would. He would rave on.' The point here, however − and in the following chapters − far from flatly being that one book or self-portrayal has directly evolved from another, is rather to suggest that the lines of literary force transecting both, and to some degree delineating a discernible period in American personal narrative, are worthy of further study. We have often said, but now perhaps have a new way in which to know, that *The Education of Henry Adams*, that 'last book' of the American nineteenth century, was really a beginning.

2

Chapters of Experience: Henry James

It had all been in truth a history — for the imagination that could take it so.

The American Scene

It is conventionally agreed that with the three great novels of his so-called 'major phase' — *The Wings of the Dove* (1902), *The Ambassadors* (1903), *The Golden Bowl* (1904) — Henry James fulfilled and in effect concluded his career as novelist, despite the fact that he lived on until 1916, most of that time in good health, and left at his death such unfinished efforts as *The Ivory Tower* and *The Sense of the Past*. It is also conventionally assumed that James's three avowedly autobiographical volumes — *A Small Boy and Others* (1913), *Notes of a Son and Brother* (1914), *The Middle Years* (1917) — constitute his only deliberate gesture toward autobiography as such, the incompleteness of which (the record breaks off in the mid-1870s at the 'end' of the unfinished third book) is to be understood in terms of a life already in effect fully shaped and interpreted through a completed career in art. Whatever the inevitable frequencies with which the novelist employed autobiographical material, or the autobiographer employed novelistic procedure, these two concentrated bursts of narrative energy are taken as separate culminations, artistic and autobiographical, to James's literary life.

Thus stated, however, this view tends also to reinforce certain conventional assumptions concerning *The American Scene*, the account James published in 1907 of his visit to the United States in 1904–5, after a quarter-century of absence, his only full-length

16

narrative published after the novels of 1902–4 and before the autobiographies of 1913–17. These assumptions are both less accurate and less innocuous in their critical convenience than those concerning the late fiction and the formal autobiography, and may be summarized as follows. However delicately James may have recorded his impressions, or registered the 'character' of situations in which he places himself as a protagonist of sorts; however astute may have been his sense of the symbolic value as cultural portents of certain features of the immediate American scene; the work as a whole is nonetheless to be read as a casually connected series of travel reminiscences, without additional imaginative design or documentary coherence. Moreover, it is said, as 'personal narrative' the book is randomly and often obscurely reflective, rather than in any systematic sense autobiographical. And in any case this volume is generally regarded as incomplete, since a planned sequel, to deal with the Western portion of James's trip, was never executed.

On the contrary, *The American Scene* (which James first envisioned as a novel in his established mode with an American setting) may usefully be considered as a kind of novel, in which an author-protagonist re-enacts through interlocking and accumulating 'scenes' the journeys of interior discovery undertaken by his fictional protagonists, within an exterior context of a collision of cultures. These scenes, or 'chapters of experience' as James refers to them at one point, consist of meditative moments dramatically developed, with James as his own 'lucid reflector' at the center of each sequence. The significance of each sequence, be it personal or historical, is discovered by James's persona and revealed to the reader in an imaginative event – a 'chapter' within a larger 'story' – and expressed in a corresponding vocabulary. *The American Scene* contains, indeed, much the same sort of self-scrutiny as to representational method, and much the same sort of language with respect to literary 'values,' as the Prefaces James began writing for the New York Edition of the novels as he was completing this book.

The American Scene is also what it more explicitly purports to be: a selective but purposeful documentary 'report' on American conditions ca. 1905, culminating in a vision, prophetic and elegaic, of American cultural prospect and retrospect. The commentary contained in this vision is far from a mere restatement of James's earlier objection to America's lack of historical atmosphere.

It stems rather from the cumulative experience, within the book's development, of James's 'restless analyst' (as he calls himself throughout), a persona sharply similar in many ways to Henry Adams's self-portrayal in the *Education*, which was privately circulated in the same year James's volume appeared.

The American Scene is finally, in a sense fusing its imaginative and documentary aspects, a methodical rather than incidental work of autobiography, in which James repeatedly brings the remembered or reimagined past to bear on the present moment of his encounter with an altered America. Through the tracing of autobiographical continuities between past and present, through the linking of his personal history with the places and events about which he writes, he seeks to deal with a sense of personal and literary discontinuity — with reawakened questions concerning his identity as an American, and about the ways in which he as a writer should engage new American material. Such questions are unexpected in their intensity, to an American by now long-settled in Europe, and to a writer already certain of the wholeness of his achievement in the art of the novel. In contending with these questions, James arrives at a sense of closure to the record of his relation to his native land, which neither his culminating novels nor his unfinished regular autobiography can as effectively supply.

The book, then, is in several ways about its own composition and its own composer, as well as about — as a *way* of being about — its more literal subjects. James distinguishes the inward from the outward eye, an 'artistic' from a 'transcriptive' accuracy, yet insists on their fusion throughout. He distinguishes a 'caring' from a more neutral attitude toward his material, yet insists on their fusion in the 'intimate intelligence' to which he here aspires. Such 'fusion,' indeed — taken also in the sense of the blending of impressions from different times during 1904–5 and from the distant past, of the blending of these in turn with the thoughts generated by the actual writing during 1905–7 — acquires through James's frequent use of the term the force of compositional principle. He inquires into, even as he asserts, the legitimacy of mixing the 'documentary' with the 'imaginative,' the 'historical' with the 'novelistic,' the 'critical' with the 'aesthetic.' But both distinctions among and interchangeable uses of such concepts recurrently pave the way to the main issue for James: *in*fusion of himself into his material, and enactment of his restless analyst's 'detached' yet 'proximate' role.

The opening chapter, 'New England: An Autumn Impression,' consists in its opening pages of evocations of 'Arcadian' repose. The 'New England Arcadia' — to which James quickly repaired upon arriving in New York from England, as if more truly to launch a voyage of rediscovery from such surroundings — is an idyllic landscape of 'nestled nooks and shallow, carpeted dells,' with 'outlooks to purple crag and blue horizon.' James's descriptions at this point are in fact abstract compositions, which make of Arcadia an imaginative rather than a literal place: 'When you wander about in Arcadia you ask as few questions as possible. That *is* Arcadia in fact,' a restful condition of aesthetic satisfaction and security.

A reader soon sees these picturings of 'autumnal harmony' in New Hampshire as referring more importantly to this state of self-composure than to the actual fulfillments of the season in nature and local life. For James

> the memory of a characteristic perfection attaches, I find, to certain hours of declining day spent, in a shallow cove, on a fallen log, by the scarce-heard plash of the largest liquid expanse under Chocorua; a situation interfused with every properest item of sunset and evening star, of darkened circle of forest, of boat that, across the water, put noiselessly out — of analogy, in short, with every typical triumph of the American landscape 'school' . . . .[1]

He luxuriates in the landscape-school conventions, even as he goes on to note their 'cruel variance' from other, more direct observations. And his diction correspondingly heightens 'not the actual, current, impeachable, but the old ideal and classic' types of which the scene is composed. Regarding the picture from without, yet also appearing as a motionless figure within it (a strategy he frequently adopts), James finds that 'that boat across the water is safe, sustaining as far as it goes.' In Arcadia one need go no further.

Yet in so far as this and other similarly 'framed' moments, occurring early in the narrative, are more expressive of an inner mood than descriptive of an actual scene, they contain a certain ambiguity. The recurrent note of reluctance to leave Arcadia suggests a need to do just that, an interrogative impulse at odds with the 'perfection' of James's self-enclosure within a landscape-school composition. The unrepresented farther shore of the Chocorua lake takes on in this light a new meaning as imaginative destination: an 'actual, current' America beyond 'that boat's' sustaining range, and requiring another sort of narrative frame. Lingering in Arcadia, inventing for it continuities with its classical literary and pictorial types, James is nonetheless increasingly aware of 'questions,' 'puzzles,' 'mysteries' inherent in the immediate rather than the mythicized situation. They disturb his Arcadian calm, but they also stimulate the 'restlessness' of his imaginative exposure and response to his actual surroundings. And they are to some extent literary questions, puzzles, mysteries; problems of representational response having less to do with James's literal observations of 1904–5 than with the process of an author-protagonist's absorption of those observations at this stage of the narrative.

These concerns – through exploration of which a restless analyst might eventually *re*compose a relation between his past and present as an American, between the past and envisioned future of America itself – draw from James's emerging persona a different depiction of his relation to an American scene. He finds himself

> before each scene, wish really to get *into* the picture, to cross, as it were, the threshold of the frame. It never lifts, verily, this obsession of the story-seeker, however often it may flutter its wings, it may bruise its breast, against surfaces either too hard or too blank.[2]

Now thinking more in a novelist's than in a landscape painter's terms, seeking to unfold a story rather than to present a completed picture, James emphasizes the effort, even the violent struggle of the imagination to penetrate resistant, unarticulated material, rather than its noiseless drift across the perfectly composed surface of the previous scene.

Another pair of passages may both broaden and refine the point. In the Saco Valley farmlands, James sees 'the semblance of a sacred grove' within

> those great fields of standing Indian corn which make, to the eye, so perfect a note for the rest of the American rural picture, throwing the conditions back as far as our past permits, rather than forward, as so many other things do, into the age to come.[3]

The scene 'lighted the way to the great modern farm,' yet the thrust of its 'general meaning' is altogether toward a timelessly pastoral effect, a removal from history into eternal Autumn which soothes the restless analyst 'perfectly to peace.' James's treatment of the 'classical abandoned farm' of the region, however, far from removing it from history, transcribes into his narrative its 'hard little historic record of agricultural failure and defeat,' which is both the more representative and the more current truth. If the scene along the Saco throws a reader's mind back to Keats's 'Ode to Autumn,' these

.

> scenes of old, hard New England effort, defeated by the soil and the climate and reclaimed by nature and time — the crumpled, lonely chimney-stack, the overgrown threshold, the dried-up well, the cart-track vague and lost[4]

send the mind forward to Frost's 'Directive.' Just as the first passage pre-empts the analyst's task by absorbing him into the generalized image of the past, so this one accentuates his role, by drawing him briefly into reflection on the past life of a more particular place, in order to refocus his attention on the present. The picturesque is still sought, with 'every properest item' (as with the lake near Chocorua) duly catalogued. But the movement .of James's imagination is back toward a more painful present from within the idyllic aspect of the scene, just as in Frost's poem the reader is 'directed' toward self-encounter in the present through strategic self-loss in the past. Wholeness beyond confusion is beside the central point (as indeed in 'Directive') — the confusions of the 'tangled [American] actual,' to which James's mind returns from this reverie, are in the process of becoming his main subject in the book. This sequence, which at first appears to be the more retrospective of the two, is in fact the one redirecting him more purposefully, less peacefully, toward the problem of his own relationship to the American 'age to come.'

The New England chapter as a whole plays out variations on these Arcadian and anti-Arcadian themes, at once activated by and analytical of the tension between these modes of the author-protagonist's consciousness. In Cambridge, walking through Harvard Yard, James registers a general impression of changelessness within, and of 'great change' without, the Yard's preserving walls. A reassuring image of the university as a 'life-saving monastery of the dark ages' mixes with a contrasting one of an institution 'massed there in multiplied forms, with new and strange architectures looming through the dark,' (James converging for the moment with both Adams and Aquarius). Even while he relishes the 'cloistered' atmosphere, indulges 'the instinct not to press, not to push on, till forced, through any half-open door of the real' world beyond the gates, the episode is concluding with his sense of the insistence of that reality, of being forced into its 'multitudinous modern hum' by way of his ongoing narrative. The entire scene is a 'brief idyll,' but the idyll's rupture is the scene's culminating effect.

Similarly, passing the Lowell and Longfellow houses on his way to the James family gravesites in Mount Auburn Cemetery, he imagines himself on

a builded breakwater against the assault of matters demanding a *literal* notation. I walked, at the best, but on the breakwater – looking down, if one would, over the flood of the real, but much more occupied with the sight of old Cambridge ghosts,[5]

the ghosts of friends and family, especially in a notebook passage James withheld as too painfully personal, ghostly traces of which appear in the published text.[6] If James is Strether-like in his double sense of Harvard, and in his sense of pressured passage from one world into another, he is here a 'revisiting spirit,' an 'ancient contemplative person,' just as Adams portrays a 'posthumous' self in the *Education*. But James, again like Adams, is as intent on the present and its suggestion for the future as on the past. The breakwater is imaginatively 'builded' as much for prospect out as for safe harbor within, the 'flood of the real' about to crest in four chapters to follow on New York (placed in rhetorical opposition to New England, although James gathered most of their material at the end of his American sojourn). Looking later across the river from the cemetery, musing (in the unprinted passage) over the inscription from Dante on Alice James's funeral urn, James sees (in the published version) the blank stadium walls as being by contrast 'like some flat memorial slab that waits to be inscribed' with the 'fantastic lettering' of the American future.

The onset of winter is in the very moment, autumn colors fading into a 'grim tracery of November.' Earlier, delighted by an unexpected display of French paintings in a Connecticut estate, James had described the effect as 'like the sudden trill of a nightingale, lord of the hushed evening' – a music, significantly, not actually to be heard in the American countryside. Now, with the 'breaking up' of a season so prominently associated with James's Arcadian compositions, 'everything broke, everything went – everything was transposed at least into another key.' The transposition more importantly occurs in the author-protagonist's character, in the texture of his personal response and the nature of his literary strategy, than in the mere atmosphere of reminiscence.

When James visited Chicago in 1905, a local reporter's account of his arrival cast the novelist, parodically, as a figure in one of James's own novels:

> Mr. James gave himself up to the little dreary pictures of Chicago life, which framed themselves on either hand in the square of cab door glass. It came home to him in the orthodox Jamesian manner that all he had heard of Chicago was stock-yards and boards of trade and dirt and coarse fearful exploits in the getting of money.[7]

At the outset of 'New York Revisited,' James presents himself through a similar strategy, if in a different mood, on approach to a city he had once known well. He begins with a moment not part of a visit to the city at all, but rather of 'circumnavigation' around it on a train-carrying barge so as to avoid 'pushing through the terrible town' on a trip from Washington to Boston. Thus the pictures he initially selects frame themselves in the square of Pullman window glass, pass before him 'without arrest or confusion' as he looks out on the 'whirlpool' of New York, toward the vortex of which he nonetheless feels himself drawn.

He considers as a theoretical topic his self-investment in the developing situation, choosing (as often throughout) economic metaphors which connect his interest here in the scale and power of American wealth with his interest as a novelist in the moral as well as the monetary cost. New York is to James the primary expression of the new American age, the relation of which to the nineteenth century (suddenly felt as an 'antique' era in personal and cultural history, much as Adams felt the twentieth century being launched ca. 1865) he can explore only in terms of his 'own more or less immediate presence' – cultural transformation thus accessible through personal revaluation of changes observed. 'History is never, in any rich sense, the immediate crudity of what "happens," but the much finer complexity of what we read into it and think of in connection with it. If . . . an incident ministered on the spot to a boundless evocation, it then became history of a splendid order.' Cited here as a principle of historical analysis, this is also in effect a principle of narrative composition, rooted in an author's sense of himself as an actor in, as well as architect of, the 'drama' (one might as easily say 'novel') of return to his native land.

Hence, circling the city in his barge-borne train (the mode of transport itself seeming to fuse two eras), James feels 'memory and the actual impression' fuse briefly into a simultaneous sense of visits distant and recent, during winter and summer. But this harmonized image begins immediately to break up into longer passages which, like the 'monstrous' urban energies James senses across the bay, 'grow and grow' toward domination of the narrative in terms more prophetic than retrospective:

> One has the sense that the monster grows and grows . . . ; the future complexity of the web, all under the sky and over the sea, becoming thus that of some colossal set of clockworks, some steelsouled machine-room of brandished arms and hammering fists and opening and closing jaws. The immeasurable bridges are but as the horizontal sheaths of pistons working at high pressure, day and night, and subject, one apprehends, with perhaps inconsistent gloom, to certain, to fantastic, to merciless multiplication.[8]

Such 'apprehension,' in both its senses, is in fact more consistent than otherwise with James's treatment, as he abandons the viewpoint afforded by the barge, and moves closer to city scenes the 'vehemence' of which calls forth a corresponding intensity of response.

Skyscrapers, from offshore a 'vast bristling promontory,' more closely viewed reflect 'the consciousness of the finite, the menaced, the essentially *invented* state, [which] twinkles ever, to my perception, in the thousand glassy eyes of these giants.' Though menaced themselves by their lack of anchorage in aesthetic tradition, they convey to James a menace quite potent as historical force. The Trinity Church spire, 'cruelly overtopped' and no longer capable of drawing the aspiring eye, becomes for a moment the embodiment of American beauty, deprived of visibility and proper scale by 'mountainwalls' of commerce, and 'hideously threatened' as if by avalanche. Similarly Castle Garden, now 'shrunken, barely discernible' in relation to its architectural surroundings, 'outlives' itself in a remembered image of the singer Patti in concert; the cramped rotunda for a moment an expansive 'firmament of long-extinguished stars.' In each case a personal fragment of the past is superimposed on the present fact, and made to stand for an endangered or superseded 'value.' Yet in each case as well the nostalgic moment is reabsorbed into the immediate observation, which engages the author-protagonist's interest if not his sympathy, and which defines his dramatic presence, whereas sheer nostalgia tends to disperse it.

So too, describing a visit to the neighbourhood of his birth, James celebrates 'the felicities of the backward reach.' But 'escape into the past,' for a persona receiving definition from the 'pressure of the present,' is no more sustaining to his sense of narrative purpose than the present is appealing to his sense of the past as a 'value.' James's 'artful evasion of the actual' in this scene through nostalgic reverie results inevitably in renewed confrontation with the actual, and the problem of personal relation to it. The quest for the house in which he was born leads only to the spot in Washington Place it no longer occupies. The inevitability of this outcome, as in various repetitions of essentially the same pattern throughout the New York chapters, has acquired an aesthetic, a compositional 'value,' diametrically opposed to that underlying the pictorial stasis and imaginative security of James's Arcadian images. Here he finds himself, in the absence of an image he had expected to see, thrown back on his own 'field of prepared sensibility,' and restlessly resuming the self-interrogation on which his dramatic existence has come to depend. In the process he finds himself devising (while thinking aloud about the task) provisional rather than fixed narrative 'frames' through which to link, rather than within which to contain separately, the phases of his dramatic progress toward a reformulated sense of self.

His return from this venture into empty autobiographical space – space requiring to be filled by the lost connection between the 'birthhouse' and the 'towers of glass,' but which he alternatively begins to fill by dealing with broken biographical relation as the *form* of relation now pertaining to his case – brings him to the Waldorf-Astoria, a 'paradise peopled with unmistakable American shapes,' a 'realized ideal' of the American impulse toward 'perfect human felicity' in public and material forms. James's language suggests that he sees the 'hotel-world' as the modern equivalent (albeit reversed in its value for him) of New England Arcadia, a 'world whose relation to its form and medium was practically imperturbable.' But despite this association, the material of New York will not submit to Arcadian analysis. The tall buildings are 'risen by the breath of an interested passion that, restless beyond all passions, is forever seeking more pliable forms.' James offers this as an aesthetic criticism; yet in his restlessness of personal displacement he too continuously seeks, and frequently finds, more pliable forms in which to cast the 'elastic' material of America.

He becomes 'conscious of the force with which this vision of [the buildings'] prodigious working . . . may beget, on the part of the restless analyst, the impulse to describe and present the facts and express the sense of them.' Momentary shades of Whitman (for whom James expressed during this American journey an admiration matured out of earlier criticism). Shades too of Zola, to whose 'love of the human aggregation, the artificial microcosm,' James's thought goes in the face of New York's 'huge constructed and compressed communities.' Zola is invoked partly to suggest the epic possibilities in the material of the city, and partly to enable James to decline the invitation to epic treatment by distinguishing Zola's situation from his own:

> Zola's huge reflector got itself formed, after all, in a far other air; it had hung there, in essence, awaiting the scene that was to play over it, long before the scene really approached it in scale. The reflecting surfaces, of the ironic, of the epic order, suspended in the New York atmosphere, have yet to show symptoms of shining out, and the monstrous phenomena themselves, meanwhile, strike me as having, with their immense momentum, got the start, got ahead of . . . any possibility of poetic, of dramatic capture.[9]

James in one sense backs away, as often elsewhere in the book, from the issue he has raised, pleading too many impressions for too little narrative time and space. In another sense, however, he makes an implicit case − a case he has already begun to make explicit by his own experimental example − for the literary 'capture' of American phenomena in other than traditionally recognized forms. Granted that his sense of alternative form is often tentative, *con*fusing as well as fusing the documentary with the imaginative, the historical with the personal, and debating as well as assuming a kinship between such terms. 'Inquiries these, evidently, that are answerable only in the presence of the particular cases provoking them; when indeed they may hold us as under a spell.' It remains true that James goes on, throughout the volume, to 'extemporize' formally in particular cases, under the spell of personal response.

Certain aspects of his response to Boston provide an example at once representative and particularly striking. Boston is for James, as he poses the literary problem of redefining his relation to it, a '"sunk" picture,' a painting whose surface layerings have been so compacted by time that revarnishing is required to revive its original tones. (Lillian Hellman would later develop in *Pentimento*, named for the emergence of earlier forms within images later painted over, a similar sense of both the problem and the principle of personal narrative.) James's metaphor becomes mixed with that of earth strata so closely compressed around a buried object as to require an archaeologist's delicate touch for successful excavation. James's point *and* his representational problem is the fusion of his old and new impressions, with a view to making them simultaneously stand as a chapter of personal and cultural history. The visual intensities of the sunk picture are renewed, the significance overlain and altered by deposits of intervening change is exposed, old Boston is resituated in the new American scene, through attention to compactions in James's own consciousness.

He keeps nostalgic 'tryst' with the house in Ashburton Place where he lived two years at the close of the Civil War, at the outset of his literary career. (This is one of several moments which faintly yet insistently sound a note − 'full of both intimate and of public vibrations' − of relationship between the Civil War and the launching of James's life as a writer. A natural association for a writer beginning in those years; but intriguing too, in the sense that one gets of James − who paid little direct literary attention to the war − trying to recover a relation to the public experience of 1861−5, as one source of renewed private relation to the America of 1905. There is more to be said of this in connection with the chapter on Richmond.) James notes as he writes, as he did not when actually visiting the house, the 'consciousness of a possible doom' in the structure's 'face,' surrounding ground already being cleared for the 'horrific glazed perpendiculars of the future.' On the original occasion the 'effort of actual attention' had been on 'ghostly footsteps,' much as it had been in Cambridge during the New England chapter. Thus far little different from several scenes in the book of simple reminiscence. Still near the start of the sequence, however, the mood is shattered with psychic consequences more violent for the quasi-novelistic protagonist, methodological implications more pronounced for the quasi-autobiographer, and narrative ramifications more extensive for the improviser of a mixed form, than are found, say, in James's attempted escape to the past of Washington Place in New York. Returning to the same site in Boston a month later,

> I found but a gaping void, the brutal effacement, at a stroke, of every related object, of the whole precious past . . . . I had been present, by the oddest hazard, at the very last moment of the victim in whom I was most interested; the act of obliteration had been breathlessly swift, and if I had often seen how fast history could be made I had doubtless never so felt that it could be unmade still faster. It was as if the bottom had fallen out of one's own biography, and one plunged backward into space without meeting anything. That, however, seemed just to give me . . . the whole figure of my connection with everything . . . .[10]

If the old house was the victim in whom he was most interested, he is now (as he put it at the Waldorf-Astoria) 'the victim of [his own] interest' in matters from which he emotionally shrinks but to which he is intellectually — and as a dramatic presence in his own 'story' — strongly drawn. This sense of a life abruptly deprived of usual reference points, of the joint 'unmaking' of personal and cultural experience, was also felt by the other major members of James's literary generation: Howells, Clemens and, pre-eminently, Adams. They not only sensed a similar autobiographical void; they did so at similarly advanced ages, and stages of career, and during what each perceived as a period of accelerating change. Each in turn was led to reconsider his 'connection with everything,' in terms of literary resources and objectives as well as in terms of personal outlook.

In 'New England,' we learn from James's notebooks, he was determined not to 'go smash on the rock of autobiography' (and so, in a conventional gesture of impersonality, used only initials in referring to such close friends as Lowell and Howells). Here in 'Boston,' having in effect experienced an autobiographical wreck far more complicated than that he had earlier feared, the author's procedural and the protagonist's psychological problem has become one of utilizing, not merely expressing a sense of, the broken biographical basis of the new narrative situation. The 'whole figure' of James's connection with the scene has become the 'sense of rupture,' between an earlier image still echoing visually in his mind, and the 'present conditions' which obliterated it, conditions to which he has himself been with equal violence autobiographically transposed. The unmaking of one personal relation is thus the making of another, decisively different. It is also the launching of a chapter, as James's 'small cluster of early associations shrivel to a scarce discernible point' through this episode, from which point of autobiographical contraction then are redispersed the chapter's remaining scenes.

Boston is itself 'disappearing' for James, although dissolving into the 'history of something, as against the history of nothing,' which is how he here conceives the future history of New York with its immense ahistorical momentum. His vantage retracts, as if in retreat, to a point on Beacon Hill from which he looks over 'the old more definite Boston,' the lines and planes of the State House, the Common, Park Street and its church 'ruled and pencilled' into harmonious 'values.' He is 'held by the vision of the closed order which shaped itself, continually, in the light of the differing present.' The 'irresistible spell' of this vision, however, is not in the purity of that pattern, but 'something sharper yet — the coercion, positively, of feeling one's deeper discomfiture' at the failure of the imaginatively drafted design to hold. From his hilltop, surveying '"my" small homogeneous Boston of the more interesting time,' James takes the 'measure of the distance by which the general movement was away — always and everywhere, from the old presumptions and conceivabilities.' The full measure of Jamesian snobbery and aloofness toward 'the Alien' is apparent, as people speaking a 'rude form of Italian' invade the Common from the north, and the 'Irish yoke' tightens from the south. Yet the scene more importantly consists in a subtler form of historical awareness, an acceptance of personal superannuation through which comprehension rather than disapproval of change becomes the higher 'value.' Howells's Bromfield Corey, taking from the same hill a possessive 'backward view' of Boston, had experienced a similar redeeming moment of historical self-awareness in *The Rise of Silas Lapham*; Wharton had more recently infused *The House of Mirth* with a comparable sense of the passing of old New York, without ascribing it to a particular character, or resolving the ambiguity of her own attitude. Now, descending the hill, the streets stretching out below like 'telescopes' of time, James watches the new Boston in which he has no part spread into the future. The 'disconnection was complete' — the narrative consequences of the earlier 'rupture' fulfilled — and he turns again, as if stepping back into a '"sunk" picture' now restored, to

> the other, the concentrated Boston of history, . . . [which] could be seen in as definite, and indeed now in almost as picturesquely mediaeval, a concretion, appearing to make as black and minute and 'composed' a little pyramidal image, as the finished background of a Dürer print.[11]

Thus James — along with Adams — takes momentary refuge, which he knows will not long avail, from the modern in the medieval.

The 'other' direction of James's interior view from Beacon Hill, toward the 'Boston of Emerson, Thoreau, Hawthorne,' is also the direction of Concord. Concord 'had an identity more palpable to the mind . . . than any other American town,' an identity mainly traceable to the Transcendentalist 'portrait-group,' but beyond that to the 'old Concord Fight' of 1775, which James calls the 'large, firm nail, ringingly driven in,' from which that portrait was to hang. The 'field of prepared sensibility' he brings to bear on that battle — a scene of historical significance the more significant to him because its true meaning remains unspoken by 'official history' — belongs even more clearly here than in previous sequences to an author-protagonist, rather than to the original observer:

> I remember putting it to myself . . . : would one know, for one's self, what had formerly been the matter here, if one hadn't happened to be able to get round behind, in the past, as it were, and more or less understand?[12]

The 'dim, shy spectralities' of the place, Revolutionary and Trans-cendental, would themselves require some such imaginative act of a revisiting spirit before appearing to him.

'The Fight had been the hinge — so one saw it — on which the large revolving future was to turn.' Here it becomes the hinge on which the narrative opens to James's ruminations on American identity, from which the sequence flows, like the Concord River which itself 'had watched the Fight,' and into the depths of which James looks from the bridge — not seeing his reflected image, but feeling himself drawn into the current. The river in this moment fuses color and sound with the 'palpable' sense of immersion in time, a synaesthetic 'note' in which James perceives the event whose 'seriousness gave once and for all the pitch' to America's subsequent history. As the water 'seeks friction' against the river's banks, so James finds in the 'full, slow' constancy of its shifting surfaces the imaginative surface on which to record meanings 'not to be recorded' in the usual historical or literary forms. What James in the writing thus 'reads into' the scene is 'the pity and the irony of the *precluded* relation on the part of the fallen defenders,' their unconsciousness of the magnitude of the 'gift' inherent in their action:

> The sense that was theirs and that moved them we know, but we seem to know better still the sense that wasn't, and that couldn't, and that forms our luxurious heritage as our eyes, across the gulf, seek to meet their eyes . . . .[13]

Merging himself with his readers as a countryman through his 'we' (he does so often in spirit but less frequently in grammar), James struggles to know what his fictional protagonists must also struggle to discover, though fated to fail through limitations of vision: the elaborated meaning of 'the short, simple act.'

It is partly a matter of paying patriotic tribute, but beyond the question of political inheritance lies a more generalized moral concern. The defenders are precluded not only from 'conscious credit,' but also from the effort to establish conscious relation between action and consequence, between the meaning of a moment and the meaning of a life — a process on which Jamesian heroism depends. But they are also precluded from the fact of human failure in that effort, and to that extent they share — like the figures on Keats's urn — in attainment to the ideal. 'The pity and the irony' is perhaps James's closest approach, here or in fiction, to classical pity and terror. We may even feel that, whatever his stature as a tragedian of the novel, he is reading into this scene more than it can bear of tragic weight. The fact remains, however, that he makes this imaginative commitment to a documentary situation, and that here, as in the novels, the knowledge that matters remains 'inexpressible,' thus treatable only in imaginative terms. Strether's long last gaze into Marie de Vionnet's eyes reaches across a widening distance and is broken at last; the Prince and Maggie Verver are finally seen, as if diminished in perspective, with eyes averted in ambiguous embrace; 'our eyes, across the gulf, seek to meet their eyes' but finally fail. The focus is now on James's, indeed on 'our,' effort so to see. And here, as in *The Ambassadors* or *The Golden Bowl*, the effort is more valuable than the result, or rather is the only thing capable of redeeming the inevitable human result.

'Beyond even such broodings,' as if slowly resurfacing in time, James shifts back to the Concord of Emerson, 'the first, and the one really rare, American spirit in letters,' seeing something therefore 'absolute in the fact of Emerson's all but lifelong connection' with the town. It is as if James were now seeking, and finding, Emerson's eyes across the gulf. Emerson had been a frequent guest in his father's house when he was a child; he had attended Emerson's funeral in 1882, during his last visit to the United States; his concern with his fictional characters' moral use of themselves, perhaps even his projection of himself in nonfictional narrative as morally engaged participant, not simply as observer, owes something to Emerson. Concord and its environs gave Emerson, in James's view, 'his nearest vision of life, and he drew half his images, we recognize, from the revolution of its seasons . . . . It is admirably, to-day,' as James finally reawakens to the present moment in which he began by gazing into the Concord River, 'as if we were still seeing these things *in* those images' of Revolutionary and Transcendental communion.

A direct reference to the Concord sequence in a later chapter, 'Washington,' invites comparison between the processes of James's response here and at Mount Vernon. Imagination 'worked at Mount Vernon, for the restless analyst, quite as it had worked a few months before, on the small and simple scene of Concord Fight.' He begins the Washington chapter by noting the dominance of a brief springtime impression of Mount Vernon over his sense of the city proper, linked to a longer winter stay. This recollection is washed in 'rare light, half green, half golden,' a 'veil . . . which operates, for memory, quite as the explosion of spring' transforms the landscape. The veil of spring light is at once a curtain rising on an opening scene, and a medium through which the scene 'transfigures,' at its close, the 'real' Washington, to which James then returns his narrative attention.

The situation is one of 'human charm,' also of human scale, as against the 'Imperial' scale of the city's 'perpetual perspectives.' The spell is cast by Mount Vernon's (like Concord's) relative simplicity:

> The hard little facts, facts of form, of substance, of scale, facts of essential humility and exiguity, look us straight in the face, present themselves literally to be counted over — and reduce us thereby to the recognition of our supreme example of the rich interference of association. Association does, at Mount Vernon, simply what it likes with us,[14]

the artist's imagination no longer the shaping force, but itself a part of the shaped material of the scene. The feeling is one 'other than the aesthetic,' of sheer absorption into the moment and the place, with the persona's 'interference' enriching rather than disrupting the writer's subject. The question of criticism — architectural, for example, a recurrent index of James's dissatisfaction with America — is rendered irrelevant, as an interest in the structure deepens into a communion with its original occupant: 'it is not the possessive case, but the straight, serene nominative . . . . The whole thing *is* Washington' — as Concord had been Emerson — 'not his invention and his property, but his presence and his person.' As at Concord, James speaks of 'us' and 'our,' and in another expression of uncritical patriotism and sincerity of which transcends the cliché, feels 'positively wrapped' in the flag, a feeling he claims as one of present 'intellectual exaltation,' not vague nostalgia for the past. Everything 'conduces to a single great representative image,' a supremely 'American picture.' James's presence in the picture, like imaginative immersion in the Concord River, makes him feel his resumption of native relations in a way never possible without such a prelude, in a way which makes possible a richer blend of critical and sympathetic analysis of Washington. Thus an excursion from the city becomes a gateway back in, a passage also to an unfolding chapter. 'Thus we arrive,' once again as at Concord, 'at the full meaning, as it were — thus we know, at least, why we are so moved.'

James speaks in 'Philadelphia' of his impression of that city as having found, in certain details noted on arrival, 'quite the pre-figurement that the chapters of a book find in its table of contents.' One passage from 'Philadelphia' seems itself to prefigure the main concerns of James's concluding chapters — 'Richmond,' Charleston,' 'Florida.' He proclaims the human need for, and pronounces yet again the American lack of, a deep-rooted social consensus from which a collective consciousness may proceed, something ideally with 'an heroic or romantic association':

> But the difficulty is that in these later times, among such aggregations, the heroic and romantic elements, even under the earliest rude stress, have been all too tragically obscure, belonged to smothered, unwritten, almost unconscious private history; so that the central something, the social *point de repère*, has had to be extemporized rather pitifully after the fact, and made to consist of the biggest hotel [etc.][15]

The statement in context has nothing directly to do with the Civil War, the 'huge shadow' and 'ghostly presence' of which dominates the Richmond sequence. Nor is it concerned with the 'apotheosis' of the American hotel-world in Palm Beach's Royal Poinciana in the section on Florida. Throughout the final chapters, however, James looks back to the war (like Adams to Chartres), for an imaginative *point de repère*, from which then to move back into the 'differing present' and toward an uncertain future, with a re-examined sense of his responsibility to his material.

James places himself on a Richmond street corner, overlooking a prospect cloaked in unseasonal snow, as if seeking beneath that covering the sources of discrepancy between romantic expectation and the immediate impression. As in 'Boston,' but here with more pertinence to the emerging scene, he muses on the period of the war as also having been that of his coming to literary self-consciousness: 'How was the sight of Richmond not to be a potent idea . . . to a restless analyst who had become conscious of the charge involved in that title as long ago as the outbreak of the Civil War?' But his first 'interrogative' glimpses have brought him up short:

> 'This then the tragic ghost-haunted city, this the centre of the vast blood-drenched circle . . . ?' One had counted on a sort of

registered consciousness of the past, and the truth was that there appeared, for the moment, on the face of the scene, no discernible consciousness . . . . Richmond, in a word, looked to me simply blank and void.[16]

One thinks of Samuel Clemens, in *The Innocents Abroad*, considering the difference between anticipated awe and experienced emptiness at the Church of the Nativity: 'I touch, with reverent finger, the actual spot where the infant Jesus lay, but I think — nothing.' But James is less interested in satiric exploitation of such a situation, leading to exposure of pretensions to grandeur, than in recovering from it the missing sense of grandeur through imaginative recomposition. Such recomposition for him releases meanings known to be somewhere within the apparent void, not gratuitously superimposed. Reshaping as he writes the remembered scene, and resorting to economic metaphor again, he notes that 'the observer, like a fond investor, must spend on it, boldly, ingeniously, to make it pay.' And as Richmond begins to 'repay my outlay' — to respond to the active pressure of his persona's meditation — a clarified image begins to be resolved from the blankness of initial exposure:

the large, sad poorness was in itself a reference, and one by which a hundred grand historic connections were on the spot, and quite thrillingly, re-established. What was I tasting of . . . but the far consequences of things, made absolutely majestic by their weight and duration? I was tasting, mystically, of the very essence of the old Southern idea — the hugest fallacy, as it hovered there to one's backward, one's ranging vision, for which hundreds of thousands of men had ever laid down their lives.[17]

'Thus, by a turn of my hand [now, writing], or of my head [then, seeing], interest was evoked,' the *sine qua non* by James's own definition of the fictive, and here the nonfictive, art.

To be sure we see little of modern Richmond, since he sees only the war's 'epic dimness.' To be sure he remains a conscious outsider, by turns hesitant and presumptuous in approaching the Southern predicament. But the burden of Southern history becomes briefly his own, though the pressure of his presence and in occasional cadences oddly prefiguring Faulkner. No longer a revisiting spirit (James had never been here before), he is a 'haunted' figure in his own effort to record a sense of 'the social revolution the most unrecorded . . . , in proportion to its magnitude, that ever was.' The scene culminates and 'fades, it melts away,' in imagined sound as much as sight, a 'soft inward dirge over the eternal "false position"' of the South. Which brings him back to the Richmond street corner 'where he last left himself,' surer now of having 'done' his subject in this sequence, and of the relation between this literary act and his own literary origins.

Although James fails to summon Charleston's ante-bellum ghosts, the city does convey to him a sense of

the Margin, that was the name of it — the Margin by which the total of American life, huge as it already appears, is still so surrounded as to represent, for the mind's eye . . . , but a scant central flotilla huddled as for very fear of the fathomless depth of water, the too formidable future, on the so much vaster lake of the materially possible.[18]

As James travels deeper into previously unvisited territory, potentialities for good and ill seem 'submerged in the immense fluidity . . . , in the looming mass of the *more*, the more and more to come.' The forms to be imparted to such unformed historical substance by the force of historical acceleration are unknown, that question itself the 'deep sea into which the seeker for conclusions must cast his nets,' in the phrase an intimation of Mailer's prose in *Of a Fire on the Moon*. One recalls as well not only James's sense of the looming superfluities of New York, but also Adams's sense — amid the 'surge of a supersensual chaos' — of intellectual immersion in the 'deep-sea ocean.' And one feels increasingly the points of convergence between *The Education of Henry Adams* and *The American Scene*, both about to be issued, the one no less deliberately for all its 'privacy' of initial circulation than the other; convergence with respect to the preoccupations of a persona, and to the creation in each case of an improvisationally mixed genre.

A way station on the Pullman route from Richmond to Florida, Charleston is also a checkpoint in time between past and future. For if Charleston gives James a vague sense of 'the Margin,' Florida *is* for him 'Marginal' America, its formlessness now its articulated form, like the meaningless meaning of a beast in the jungle. 'On a strip of sand between the sea and the jungle' stand the Palm Beach hotels which loom throughout the chapter, simultaneously embodying vast material possibility and its foreclosure through a failure of historical vision. Sixty years later Mailer would begin *Miami and the Siege of Chicago* with an almost identical image of Miami Beach (set in 1915, ten years after James's visit) as a marginal settlement extravagantly 'called a city, nine-tenths jungle. An island.' While traveling south, James had imagined the softening of the landscape as an inward shift from Puritan to Pagan sensibility, his trip 'less a journey through space than a retracing of the . . . ages.' Entering Florida, he had relished the 'exquisite sense of the dream come true,' delighted in the 'velvet air' and 'citron blooms' of an atmosphere fused with that of 'Naples or Genoa.'

It is his final evocation of an imaginative Arcadia, linking his earliest and most reassuring memories of New England with the assault of immediate impressions in Florida. But Florida's Arcadian 'radiance' conceals a 'betrayal,' and as the chapter expands from this core of association and cross-reference to earlier sections, James feels

> the great sphere of the hotel close round one, covering one in as with high, shining crystal walls, stretching beneath one's feet an immeasurable polished level, revealing itself in short as, for the time, for the place, the very order of nature and the very form, the only one, of the habitable world.[19]

The Waldorf-Astoria, to which he then refers (casting a net back over 'interlinked appearances' to be gathered toward conclusion), had to his mind 'prescribed this revel,' determined powerfully the quality of life to be lived within this new order of American nature, whether in New York or Florida. But here at the height of the 'economic revel' in Florida, all prospect of an aesthetic one to match, an outreaching of American vision on the scale of American wealth, seems over, to 'fade, . . . to leave not a wreck behind.'

James has presumed in *The American Scene* – both as author and as protagonist – to creative power something like that of Prospero, to whose speech in *The Tempest* he here imperfectly but appropriately alludes. Scenes of imaginative order are strewn like islands through James's text, islands he has dramatically inhabited as well as narrationally charted. He still seems to speak from such presumption to power, involving as it does an acknowledgment of human limits, in acknowledging now the failure of a full vision of the American future to cohere. In part he dissociates himself from this failure through his familiar 'European's' judgment against the American historical atmosphere: 'Its pressure and power have failed of some weight . . . for the complexity of a scene.' He also, however, identifies more deeply with America's failure to generate forms other than those he finds in 'sole *articulate* possession,' such as the hotels. The restless analyst's 'last question' is spoken as much out of native desire, intense if disillusioned, as out of an expatriate's critical detachment: 'Is that to be, possibly, the American future,' that with such powers of 'space, of wealth, of faith and knowledge and curiosity, . . . even of sustained passion,' it will still compromise its best aspirations, which '*shall* have to continue to be represented, indefinitely, but by a gilded yearning?'

James's 'last answer' (its pressure and power sufficient to articulate the form of this complex scene) is rather an image through which this book concludes, as do most of his novels, with both author's voice and protagonist's thought informed by the calm of expended force, with the deepest ambiguities embedded in each nonetheless unresolved. Gazing at 'glimmers' of ideal possibility, knowing also the impossibility of the ideal, he arrives at a vision similar to that 'of the old island . . . that flowered once for Dutch sailors' eyes,' in which Gatsby's capacity for wonder, and Nick's consciousness of it, are fused. James too experiences a 'transitory enchanted moment,' holds his breath 'in the presence of this continent.' Florida's palm-lined shore suddenly becomes the Nile, in a scene of 'greater antiquity' than even the Sphinx,

> the antiquity of the infinite *previous*, of the time before the Pharaohs and the Pyramids, when everything was still to come.[20]

When everything has come and gone as well, for the moment is enclosed in a sense of the 'possible' foredoomed, the 'retrievable' unretrieved.

It is a moment of uncharacteristic awe, as well as one of more familiarly ironic Jamesian mood, 'the pity and the irony' (perhaps the 'pity and dread' of *The Golden Bowl*) again conjoined. But the sense of personal transfixion by the magnitude of American opportunity lost — and not inconceivably of James's own lost opportunities as an American artist 'of the epic order' — is also his deepest tribute to his national origin. It runs deeper still than the communions at Concord and Mount Vernon with America's political and literary past. Only James's communion in the opening chapter with the familial past at the Mount Auburn graveside, where his quest for a new relation to the national present may be said to begin, is as charged with jointly personal and historical verdict. That scene's significance, submerged at that point by the effort not to 'go smash on the rock of autobiography,' resurfaces in this scene's culmination of an author-protagonist's quest, the meaning of which has turned out after all to reside in an essentially autobiographical act. In accounting for James's failure to complete his formal autobiography, Leon Edel states that James

> had achieved solitude in his art; but the subject of his art had always been family relations, and personal relations. In reality there was no personal autobiography that he wanted to write, once removed from Family.[21]

The American Scene, at the outset of which James re-encountered the ghosts of Family, *is* in reality — in close connection with immediate American facts as well as the ghostly past — the personal autobiography James found he wanted to write, whatever his subsequent efforts in a more traditionally prescribed genre. It enables him to reach out from, without violating, the solitude of his art, to address American issues as an American. He does so while maintaining, at least for those moments of imaginative coalescence which constitute his 'chapters of experience,' the vantage points and the values, private and universal, of both autobiographer and artist.

Leaving Florida for the North — in 'fact' still to undertake his unwritten Western travels, but in 'truth' at book's end soon to sail East for 'home,' from the city of his birth and the land of his launching as a writer — retracing now with 'sad rigour' his imaginative journey (more like Strether once more than like Prospero), James returns to his 'proper business' as a chronicler of ordinary events. His accumulated experience as an author-protagonist, the book-long interminglings of the narrative acts of 'the journalist, the novelist, the dramatist, . . . the historian,' leave him more the 'brooding' than the restless analyst, an ostensibly exhausted figure like Adams's self-surviving persona. Seated again behind his Pullman window, seen by reader and himself alike within its receding frame, he beats the wings of his artist's frustration a final time against 'surfaces either too hard or too blank,' as he had at the out-set in New England: 'Oh for a split, a chasm, one groans beside your plate-glass, oh for an unbridgable abyss' in a continent, one feels, which has defeated James's imagination by its mass as much as by its lack of historical consecration.

Yet the mood is also one of completed engagement with a sub-ject, disengagement from which now neither nullifies positions taken nor renounces continuing concern. It is, further, one of completed re-encounter with self, the shock of recognition in 'The Jolly Corner' here attenuated and absorbed, the protagonist's withdrawal here a more self-repossessing act. It is, finally, one of enlivened interest in, more than confusion or complacency over, angles of vision afforded by experimentally aligned narrative resources and techniques, as James pulls together the varied strands of his intent, and claims the result as a unified, if still 'extempary,' method. James undergoes the transmutation of his sense of failure, by the 'symbolic agency' of the intervening plate glass, into the gentler 'ache of a question already familiar' — the self-analysis of which his fictional characters' lives, and the scenes of this book, are composed. For all the formal finality of the recently completed novels of the major phase, for all the self-shaping yet to come in the autobiographies of 1913–17, *The American Scene* as effectively as they conveys the closure of a life in art, while remaining alive to its own unexhausted possibilities. An American's search for the idea of America is here as much as there the substance of art. James's 'unfinished question' in *The American Scene* thus 'arrives easily enough, in that light, at its end.'

3
Voices from the Veil: W. E. B. DuBois to Malcolm X

Build therefore your own world.
                    Ralph Waldo Emerson, *Nature*

So why do I write, torturing myself to put it down?
                    Ralph Waldo Ellison, *Invisible Man*

En route to Florida in 1905, as he recounts in *The American Scene*, Henry James mused on the cultural 'vacancy' of the South, and wondered how 'everything [could] so have gone that the only "Southern" book of any distinction published for many a year is *The Souls of Black Folk*, by that most accomplished of members of the negro race, Mr. W. E. B. DuBois? Had the *only* focus of life then been Slavery?'[1] James's compliment to DuBois (whose book had appeared in 1903), not to mention his view of Southern culture, was oblique and condescending. But an image occurring at this point in *The American Scene* — of an empty yet still-echoing slave cell, in which are heard dissonant sounds from 'the other time' — recognizes more directly the overriding feature of the narrative sensibility of *The Souls of Black Folk*. For DuBois in this work, the focus of life *is* indeed the continuing reverberation in individual consciousness of a race's subjugation in another time. So too, in a range of subsequent works by black American authors such as Richard Wright, James Baldwin and Malcolm X, narrative consciousness of the personal present is both invaded and informed, threatened and sustained, by a sense of dissolution within the racial past.

41

'The problem of the twentieth century is the problem of the color-line,' says DuBois, '1900' to him as critical a symbolic juncture as Henry Adams would soon claim, for different reasons, in his *Education*. The problem shared with DuBois by Wright, Baldwin, Malcolm X and others is that of voicing black self-consciousness so as to create it, or to recreate it in the context of twentieth-century America. At the common core of *Black Boy, Notes of a Native Son* and *The Autobiography of Malcolm X* in addition to *The Souls of Black Folk* — granting crucial differences among them — is the urge to articulate, as if for the first time, a sensibility at once determined and precluded by history. The same urge is felt in, and is itself a subject of, such novels as James Weldon Johnson's *The Autobiography of an Ex-Coloured Man* and Ralph Ellison's *Invisible Man*. Never fully possessed of what Baldwin calls the 'white centuries' of European culture, dispossessed as well of the African past, the Afro-American protagonists in these works, whether fictional or autobiographical personae, project themselves in terms of both being and nothingness. They imagine their lives as both shaped and negated by historical pressures rooted in race, as lives in a way over before begun. Yet they also envision their individualities as unformed, and therefore open to unbounded possibility residing in personal energies compressed and awaiting release.

Loss of experience thus tends to become the experience to be depicted, as those denied by history feel themselves becoming abstractly historical: 'shadows, self-created' in Baldwin's phrase, 'empty' to Wright in a sense of more-than-physical hunger, 'posthumous' in the sense of Malcolm's certainty of assassination, 'invisible' in the many meanings of Ellison's term. From within such images of self-erasure, however — points of mental retraction 'underground' such as that from which Ellison's narrator promises powerfully to emerge — experience may also be originally discovered, as much as recovered. An autobiographical act, or an act of self-narration in a work of fiction, tends in these books to be an effort to reinitiate rather than to reflect on one's experience, to traject rather than to trace a life. It is an effort to establish a voice in which to speak oneself into being, through words to enter the world from which one feels oneself an exile since long before one's personal birth. The sense of urgency about most such efforts suggests the close proximity between the issues of literal, and literary, survival. Questing for human individuality, identifying the personal with the race's general condition, believing that while this condition persists it will be America's national condition as well, claiming a representative role not only in relation to American blacks but also in relation to the idea of America — on each level, for these self-narrators, the human predicament and the compositional problem are essentially one.

Before each chapter of *The Souls of Black Folk* stands a wordless bar of music from what DuBois calls the 'Sorrow Songs,' a 'haunting echo' of the language in which 'the slave spoke to the world.' This language was 'naturally veiled and half-articulate,' since original words and music 'lost each other' in beginning to find new Afro-American forms. It was also filled with 'eloquent omissions and silences,' expressive of the fear DuBois says always 'shadowed' the slaves' inner thoughts and relations with one another, but also expressive of the need to articulate — from within the Veil (as he calls it) of race — a sensibility isolated from the culture into which it was violently forced. An ageless tale thus requires retelling because in a sense a song without words, its omissions and silences imposed by the oppressors and strategically invented by the oppressed, parts of the self-expressive act from which they are missing. Woven into the fabric of DuBois's prose, the musical notations come to constitute emblems — resonant also in relation to Wright, Baldwin and Macolm X — of the problem of projecting in personal narrative what DuBois terms the 'strange meaning of being black here at the dawning of the Twentieth Century.'

DuBois presents *The Souls of Black Folk* as a series of essays on the political, educational and economic conditions of black Americans ca. 1900, casually intermixed with personal reflection and reminiscence. He pursues his documentary purpose, however, as an author-protagonist in whom the personal and the national predicaments are systematically united. He offers his own voice as representative, monitoring tensions within himself traceable to denial of his ancestors' selfhood, and projecting them as paradigmatic of a people's historical experience and current situation in 'this American world, — a world which yields him no true self-consciousness':

It is a peculiar sensation, this double-consciousness, this sense of always looking at one's self through the eyes of others . . . . One

ever feels his twoness, − an American, a Negro; two souls, two thoughts, two unreconciled strivings . . . .
    The history of the American Negro is the history of this strife.[2]

The powers of the black artist have been 'strangely wasted, dispersed' by the effort to resolve this double image of himself. At its core the problem is thus essentially autobiographical: a sense of powerlessness to speak in words commensurate with his experience, to an audience of which he is unsure:

> Throughout history, the powers of single black men flash here and there like falling stars, and die sometimes before the world has rightly gauged their brightness. Here in America, in the few days since Emancipation, the black man's turning hither and thither in hesitant and doubtful striving has often made his very strength to lose effectiveness, to seem like the absence of power, like weakness. And yet it is not weakness, − it is the contradiction of double aims, . . . confusion and doubt in the soul of the black artist; for the beauty revealed to him was the soul-beauty of a race which his larger audience despised, and he could not articulate the message of another people.[3]

DuBois had breached the Veil by mastering the intellectual and literary systems of the established culture through studies first at Fisk and later at Harvard and in Europe. On one level he seems to speak from beyond the dilemma he here describes − like the 'ancient contemplative' persona of James − released yet also isolated from the struggle, aged by abstract wisdom concerning conflicts unresolved in human fact, already (at thirty-five in 1903) a 'fallen star' himself. On the whole, however, he speaks from the center of the problematical situation he projects, identifying directly with the black artist as he has defined him.
    The effect of his embodiment in himself of the book's issues is one of internal and external pressures building toward some point of simultaneous opportunity and danger. He emphasizes the hope of reconciliation between black and white. But social science, as grounds for such hope, shades into language more expressive of the longing for justice 'in some fair world beyond' found in the sorrow songs: 'anon in His good time America shall rend the Veil.' The *modern* message latent in the suppressed energy of black

consciousness, eloquent only in the silences within the sorrow songs, contains in DuBois's view a 'warning' as well as an urge toward American brotherhood, in violence perhaps a form of fulfillment. In a preface written in 1953 for the Jubilee Edition of his work, DuBois clearly considers it a warning still unheeded. By positioning himself, Adams-like, at the intersection of convergent social and psychological forces, DuBois also adds a literary dimension to the sense of gathering crisis. The language and form of the sermon and the scholarly article give way at crucial moments to the need, of which the narrative is self-conscious, for alternative forms not yet available. In their wordlessness, the musical phrases at the head of each section overpower the literary epigraphs from such as Lowell and Whittier, alerting the reader to what DuBois hints are his book's 'buried' features.

Between the 'Gentle Reader' addressed in the prefatory 'Forethought,' conceived of as white and in need of reminding that the color-line restricts the lives of all, and 'God the Reader' invoked in an 'Afterthought,' that the book may be heard by 'a guilty people,' exists for DuBois a potential American readership transcending race. This audience is unable to hear fully what DuBois by his own statement cannot yet completely say. Such readers call still, in order to be brought into being, for writers in whom the contradiction of double aims is resolved. DuBois presents himself in relation to this call, less as a Whitman in relation to Emerson's famous greeting, than as a bearer of the impulse – old yet still nascent, and not unrelated to Whitman's self-procreant urge – toward black self-creation through self-articulation.

DuBois's first-born had died in infancy (as had Emerson's), and he sees in his son's fate ('Not dead, but escaped; not bond, but free') an image of his own and his nation's need to see through and thus 'rend' the Veil. His chapter on the boy's death, and his prayer to God the Reader that 'my book fall not still-born,' furnish a fallen star with life, renewing in its radiance the stars of black genius fallen throughout history, re-endowing them with the potentiality of Thoreau's 'morning star,' a sun shining on black and white alike. As this image both concludes and recommences *Walden*, so on DuBois's last page the 'weary traveller' of the sorrow songs 'sets his face toward the Morning, and goes his way.'

The path before him lies back within the book. He associates his growth as a writer with the process through which self-examination has 'changed the child of Emancipation to the youth with dawning self-consciousness':

> In those sombre forests of his striving his own soul rose before him, and he saw himself, — darkly as through a veil; and yet he saw in himself some faint revelation of his power, of his mission. He began to have a dim feeling that, to attain his place in the world, he must be himself, and not another.[4]

Ironically yet appropriately, the passage occurs in the first chapter, whereas in the last the revelation of literary power in the world is tinged with vaguer hope in divine revelation hereafter. The image of interior dawn thus gives rise to a comprehensive autobiographical act, and makes of *The Souls of Black Folk* the first movement in a modern song of myself.

In his novel *The Autobiography of an Ex-Coloured Man* (1912), Johnson's first-person narrator notes 'the opportunity of the future Negro novelist and poet to give the country something new and unknown, in depicting the life, the ambitions, the struggles, and the passions of those of their race who are striving to break the narrow limits of tradition. A beginning has already been made in that remarkable book by Dr DuBois, *The Souls of Black Folk*.'[5] Johnson's novel is an effort to exploit this opportunity, by examining his protagonist's failure to do so.

The narrator's own words declare the book's attempt at full depiction of black Americans' inner lives to be unrealized. To him, as to DuBois, it remains for a future writer to complete the literary act. One of the reasons is that the narrator — a musician — chooses to pass for white, and abandons his opportunity to express himself in art. He had blended 'classic' and 'modern rag-time,' also incorporating 'the old slave songs — material which no one had yet touched,' and which DuBois had called the only truly American music. As black, he is able only in Europe to feel American, and to find his music accepted as an expression of that identity. As 'white,' he feels compelled to seek American 'success, and that, if it can be summed up in any one word, means "money."' He defends his decision on grounds of his children's future, and a notion of integrity lying deeper than race: 'I would neither disclaim the black race nor claim the white race; but . . . let the world take me for what it would.' But he knows at the end that he has lost his essential self. His music remains unwritten, and throughout the book he withholds from us his name.

In calling his novel the autobiography of someone who in a sense no longer exists — 'Sometimes it seems to me that I have never really been a Negro, that I have been only a privileged spectator of their inner life,' says the narrator at the close — Johnson commits the resources of the novel to a specialized autobiographical purpose. This is not to say that the novel's incidents resemble those of Johnson's life, any more than DuBois chronicles his actual experience. It is to say that Johnson recognizes in his title what DuBois acknowledged in his narrative mode, fusing in the personal both documentary and story-telling voices. Only by filtering up through the experience of the race can the story of the individual transcend its racial terms. As Wright says in *Black Boy*, 'I had to feel and think out each tiny item of racial experience in the light of the whole race problem, and to each item I brought the whole of my life.' As Baldwin observes in *Notes of a Native Son*, masking in philosophical abstraction a personal intensity equivalent to Wright's, 'We cannot escape our origins, however hard we try, those origins which contain the key — could we but find it — to all that we later become.'

Racially invisible and artistically inaudible as he chooses to become, the speaker in *The Autobiography of an Ex-Coloured Man* suggests the intricacy of self-improvisation within the larger orchestration of racial identity. 'I know that in writing the following pages I am divulging the great secret of my life,' he says at the outset. That opening sentence dissolves as much as it develops into the 'vague feeling of unsatisfaction' which is the burden of the book's final paragraph, the 'lesser part' which the potentialities of his being have become. If for Baldwin the 'making of an American begins at that point where he himself rejects all other ties, any other history,' Johnson records the unmaking of that American, a process beginning and ending in that rejection. The narrator's sense of his accumulated experience is inseparable from a sense of the annihilation of that experience, its substance in emptiness, its eloquence in silence. Thus Johnson reconcentrates, more than he resolves, DuBois's double image of the black artist. He makes the artist an autobiographer as well, thus recovering in personal narrative the consciousness shown fictionally to be irrecoverable. He also sets a pattern of unresolved ambiguity between personal narrative and the novel as form appropriate to the experience he wishes to convey. This pattern is variously apparent in the work of Wright and Baldwin.

In *Black Boy* (1945) and *American Hunger* (written as part of the former but published posthumously in 1977), Wright reviews his early years with increasing emphasis on his effort to become a writer, and on the act of writing as the way to become oneself. *Black Boy* ends in 1927, with the eighteen-year-old Wright leaving the South for Chicago, seeking relief from the 'pressure of southern living' which had made it seem impossible 'to be real.' He sees in the negative act – 'running more away from something than toward something' – the only form of counter-pressure, of positive self-assertion, afforded by the confining circumstances of his life to date. *American Hunger* ends in 1937, with Wright leaving the Communist Party, and launching a literary quest for self-fulfillment, and for fulfillment of the social values which had drawn him into politics.

His discovery of books toward the end of *Black Boy*, and his own first attempts to express himself in writing, give him an exhilarating sense of life's possibilities. Reading, however, also engenders a depressing sense of isolation from those possibilities, a 'vast sense of distance between me and the world in which I lived' or about which he read. Finding no basis for 'belief in myself' in either a crushing immediate environment or an alien world beyond (the pressure of northern living if anything greater than what he experienced before), he feels his personal existence driven deep within his mind. Incandescent under pressure and 'volatile' in anticipation of violence, consciousness threatens to explode, writing as well as northward flight an effort to retard, yet also to direct, that release of energy. Consciousness is also, however, an emptiness into which he feels himself disappearing: 'I held my life in my mind, . . . feeling at times that I would stumble and drop it, spill it forever.' The demands of daily survival are such that to write might be to leak one's own force inward, just as the 'secret' of Johnson's narrator, once divulged, is known long since to have dwindled away. The closing paragraphs of *Black Boy*'s penultimate chapter are full of such contrary yet interpenetrating images, and the inward crisis they project ends the book more effectively than the final chapter, most of which Wright wrote after separating what is now *American Hunger* from the manuscript. That crisis — the essence of which is that it is unsustainable for long — is also a crisis of sustainable literary form, for the youth struggling to write in 1927 and for the author seeking a point of autobiographical completion in 1945.

American Hunger, while advancing the chronological narrative, reprojects without altering this crisis. With increasing literary experience comes a stronger sense of writing as 'significant living.' With increasing political sophistication comes a sharper sense of the problem of relation between imaginative expression and social action, between prospects for personal fulfillment in America and for America's fulfillment of its social promise. As Wright outgrows the Party without rejecting its ideals, he reabsorbs its systems of thought into his still-unsystematized literary program, his political experience finally a metaphor of incomplete relation between inner and outer realities. Verbal fragments of the Internationale are absorbed in essential meaning, if not in diction or cadence, into the sense of American racial predicament punctuated by DuBois with musical fragments from the spirituals. These words of collective aspiration, in the last pages of *American Hunger*, rejoin the tonalities of Wright's personal isolation, as music and words of the sorrow songs began to find each other again in the final pages of *The Souls of Black Folk*.

But Wright's situation as protagonist is unchanged. He looks in the last paragraph into an unformed future — 'I would hurl words into this darkness and wait for an echo.' The persona is still dominated by a sense of unbearable pressure from without, countered only by the pressure of feelings within demanding but not yet finding commensurate expression, and thus suffused with rage. The persona is still immersed in a sense of precarious fluidity, 'float[ing] loosely within the walls of my consciousness,' yet risking self-dispersal by seeking to connect through those walls with the world. 'Waiting' at the end of *American Hunger*, with pencil poised over unmarked white paper, 'I wanted' — the tense is ambiguous in implication as to the outcome of the effort — 'to try to build a bridge of words between me and that world outside.' 'Leaving' at the end of *Black Boy*, he wondered in equally ambiguous grammar if 'perhaps, gradually and slowly I might learn who I was, what I might be.' In each case the literal act which completes the narrative contains a literary act which has not yet completely occurred. Also in each case, completion of the literary act is associated with Wright's psychological survival. As in *The Auto-biography of an Ex-Coloured Man*, autobiographical scrutiny of a self poised between actuality and extinction rescues it from the incompletion which is part of its experience. In such striving toward self, which becomes in its intensity its own fulfillment, are both 'The Horror and the Glory' (*American Hunger*'s working title) of black experience in America.

In 1940 Wright had published *Native Son*. The novel confirmed Wright's reputation as America's leading black writer and as a major inheritor of the naturalistic tradition in fiction, thus also preparing a framework of public awareness within which *Black Boy* would be received. There is much in *Black Boy* — beyond a title similar in ironic as well as syllabic compression to that of the novel, and an epigraph mirroring the novel's from *Job* — to suggest that the 'truth' central to the autobiographer is also that sought by the novelist. As with *The Autobiography of an Ex-Coloured Man*, the point is not that fictional and actual incidents correspond. It is rather that just as Johnson's novel must call itself and function as an autobiography in order to achieve its purpose, *Black Boy* 'verifies' a fictional paradigm through which Wright in *Native Son* had sought to imagine the essence of his own, and his race's, experience.

This passage from the novel, viewed against the patterns of personal narrative traced above, illustrates the relationship:

> But what was he after? What did he want? What did he love and what did he hate? He did not know. There was something he *knew* and something he *felt*; something the *world* gave him and something he *himself* had; something spread out in *front* of him and something spread out in *back*; and never in all his life, with this black skin of his, had the two worlds . . . been together; never had he felt a sense of wholeness.[6]

Bigger Thomas, the novel's protagonist, is not Wright, though Wright tells us in his introduction to the novel that we are all Bigger. The passage condenses the continuity of Bigger's consciousness, just as all his direct utterance in the book seems compressed into his recurrent 'Goddam!' The accumulation of baffled questions, the frustration mounting in compoundings of 'something,' the spasmodic effort conveyed through italics to distinguish between the world's violent message and his own violent response — all are aspects of the character's inner condition and, distinct from that, of the novelist's technique. But the passage, altered only in point of view, might easily have come from Wright's autobiography. The stress of hate forces resolution of Bigger's conflict, in the murder through which he 'created a new world for himself.' Just as inevitably, Wright's autobiographical situation develops from the pressure of living in unreconciled worlds. This passage from *Black Boy*, adjusted in point of view, might easily have come – in a sense *does* come – from Wright's projection in *Native Son* of black entrapment in the white world:

> My tension returned, new, terrible, bitter, surging, almost too great to be contained. I no longer *felt* that the world about me was hostile, killing; I *knew* it. A million times I asked myself what I could do to save myself, and there were no answers. I seemed condemned, ringed by walls.[7]

In this light, the echo yet to be sounded by words yet to be hurled at the end of *American Hunger*, while awaited by Wright in hope, is inseparable from the 'ring of steel against steel' despairingly heard by Bigger in the last words of *Native Son*.

In Wright's long preface to the novel, 'How "Bigger" was Born,' the story has somehow spilled over its formal containments. Whereas in *Black Boy* Wright fears that consciousness, once dropped, might spill and be lost forever, the overflowing of *Native Son* into its author's introduction suggests that consciousness, once poured into prose, might spill forever on the page, whole volumes insufficient to stanch the flow. The narrators in *Invisible Man* and *The Autobiography of an Ex-Coloured Man* hoard the precious fluids of self, which their authors then channel – Ellison at full force and Johnson more sparingly – into narrative conduits feeding epilogue back into prologue. For Wright too (though in Ellison's words) 'the end is in the beginning and lies far ahead,' *Black Boy* and *Native Son* – bound in binary rather than chronological relation – each prologue as well as epilogue to the act of self-creation contained in the other.

Occasional parentheses in *Black Boy*, more socially analytical than the surrounding reconstructions of interior sensibility, swell in *American Hunger* into lengthier and more frequent disquisitions distinct from the flow of personal relation. One feels the autobiography pushing out of its channels of chosen literary form, blocks of documentary prose lodging in its self-imaginative stream, just as the massive blocks of 'Fear,' 'Flight' and 'Fate' displace beyond the novel narrative material still uncontained within them. One senses again the pressure of an untold story, seeking completion in contending yet complementary forms.

Wright refers to Bigger as 'a symbolic figure of American life, a figure who would hold within him the prophecy of our future,' because he is the creation, and thus the mirror image, of white America. Like DuBois before him, Wright as autobiographical protagonist also claims a representative role. For the writer more than for the apostate Communist, narrative tracing of a personal path becomes a mapping of 'history's bloody road.' Wright says in *Black Boy*, 'I feel that the Negroes' relation to America is symbolically peculiar, and from the Negroes' ultimate reactions to their trapped state a lesson can be learned about America's future.' Wright as much as Bigger holds within himself a prophecy. It awaits inscription on the blank sheets into which he stares at the close of *American Hunger*.

Baldwin's *Notes of a Native Son* (1955), as fully as any of his efforts at fictional and nonfictional analysis of racial consciousness in America, demonstrates what Alfred Kazin calls his distinguishing 'ability to turn every recital of his own life into the most urgent symbol of American crisis.'[8] Wright's sense of representative self-awareness seemed to spill out from a fictional center into autobiographical narrative still spreading (in the posthumous *American Hunger*) beyond his death. Baldwin's literary distillations of his life as an American Negro seems to have contracted from perimeters set out in his early fiction toward a center of autobiographical intensity, in narrative forms correspondingly compressed.

'Many Thousands Gone,' an essay first published in 1951 and incorporated in *Notes of a Native Son*, enlists (as had DuBois) the music of an unwritten past in the service of literary self-realization in the present. DuBois does not mention 'There's Many a Thousand Gone' as one of the 'master' sorrow songs. He might have, however, and when sung in Tod Clifton's funeral procession in *Invisible Man*, it affects the narrator much as the master songs affect DuBois. 'It was not the words, for they were all the same old slave-borne words,' says Ellison's protagonist, more dismissive of the burden of those words than DuBois had been half a century before, but drawn like DuBois into the sounds and silences beneath. It was 'something deeper' within the old music, yet also within the modern listener: 'I was listening to something within myself, and for a second I heard the shattering stroke of my heart.' Baldwin's title constitutes his only reference to the spiritual, but the phrase hovers over the narrative, in which social analysis and literary criticism become indistinguishable from autobiography, as a musical phrase presides over each section of *The Souls of Black Folk*.

Whereas Wright tended to commit the personal voice to collective statement when functioning as a representative figure — 'I feel that the Negroes' relation to American is symbolically peculiar' — Baldwin tends to pull the collective statement toward the personal, to be himself 'the Negro in America,' whom he nonetheless discusses in the third person. 'He' masks 'I,' as do 'We' and 'Our,' as Baldwin shifts in 'Many Thousands Gone' among points of identification with blacks and whites conditioned to see one another in terms of race, or with Americans he envisions (like DuBois's ideal readers) as one day able to see in terms of individuality alone. As the pronouns change orbits, ironically charged grammatical particles encircling a volatile atom of self, one senses the degree to which Baldwin is the unresolved subject of his ostensibly objective analysis.

When Baldwin says, 'What it means to be a Negro is a good deal more than this essay can discover,' he issues more than the conventional disclaimer as to scope. DuBois had said that 'to the real question, How does it feel to be a problem [instead of a person]? I answer seldom a word.' Johnson's narrator had said, from beyond the color-line, 'Concerning the position which I now hold' — meaning literally his job in real estate, but figuratively his racial status — 'I shall say nothing.' Baldwin is saying that his every word is written in answer to DuBois's question, and that more words will be required than have yet been voiced, by his or any other 'sensibility sufficiently profound and tough enough to make this tradition articulate,' to arrive at the meaning of American blackness. Whether or not (in Baldwin's words) 'It is only in his music . . . that the Negro in America has been able to tell his story,' as also suggested by DuBois, Johnson and Ellison, Baldwin here concurs with them (and with Wright) in calling it 'a story which otherwise has yet to be told and which no American is prepared to hear':

> As is the inevitable result of things unsaid, we find ourselves until today oppressed which a dangerous and reverberating silence; and the story is told, compulsively, in symbols and signs, in hieroglyphics.[9]

Baldwin, like the others, declares in the telling his tale untold, perhaps untellable in forms with which he as a writer is familiar. As with the others, the telling takes place in the reverberating silence of its own aftermath.

This is also for Baldwin the aftermath of Wright's *Native Son*, which reverberates throughout *Notes of a Native Son* as 'the most powerful . . . statement we have yet had of what it means to be a Negro in America.' He continues in 'Many Thousands Gone' to seek that meaning in terms of Wright's novel. *Black Boy* goes unmentioned, but Baldwin's remarks subsume a sense of the indirect autobiographical bond between Wright and his fictional protagonist, into which then Baldwin's own subjectivity is bound: 'no American Negro exists who does not have his private Bigger Thomas living in the skull.' The 'white-heat' in Bigger's gut, out of which he self-destructively created a new world for himself, was also the primal force in the cosmos of Wright's literary imagination. Wright spoke in *Black Boy* of feeling 'blasted' out of the world by the same ferocity of inarticulate emotion. If the novel released beyond itself the nebulae of Wright's autobiographical writing, Baldwin's essay and other of his narrative self-condensations seem also to have been launched by *Native Son*. They are dense but scattered chunks of textual matter, cooler and more intricately featured on the literary surface than their seething source, but molten at the imaginative core, pinpoints of white-heat still living in Baldwin's skull.

Baldwin objects to *Native Son* on grounds that it 'does not convey the altogether savage paradox of the American Negro's situation, of which the social reality . . . is but the shadow.' Despite the fact that it was Wright's main point, Baldwin argues it a weakness in the novel that 'Bigger has no discernible relationship to himself, to his own life, to his own people, nor to any other people.' He accurately but pejoratively locates Bigger's force in his 'incarnation of a myth' of absolute isolation. Purely literary values are no doubt at stake, the naturalist versus the psychological realist. Issues of recognition and representative responsibility are perhaps also involved, Baldwin's image as Wright's inheritor too confining in 1955, as is what Baldwin calls the 'false responsibility' of representing the race, 'thrust' on him all the same (as it had been on Wright) by autobiographical as much as public necessity. But something deeper than literary-critical or literary-political words, as something ran deeper than the slave-borne words of 'There's Many a Thousand Gone,' is more crucially involved. Baldwin laments the novel's lack of elaboration of the 'complex techniques' which American blacks, the nuances of whose lives are blotted out in *Native Son* by the mythic totality of Bigger's solitary rage, have 'evolved for their survival.' These are also the literary techniques – complex because requiring both recognition of and resistance to the meaning of Bigger, and based in the double notion that a sense of annihilation by the world is central to the act of conceiving one's place in the world – evolved by Baldwin for his own survival in self-reaffirming narrative.

'Many Thousands Gone' is thus more than an image of personal survival, one of many in the written and unwritten record of black experience in America. It too incarnates a myth, one as sacred to Baldwin as the myth of Bigger was meant by Wright to be profane, to make visible the 'moral horror of Negro life in the United States.' Baldwin incarnates his being in words, believing in their capacity, however unrealized in the individual attempt, to contain the 'vast unity' of which Wright despairs without despairing of himself in *American Hunger*. Feeling 'prohibited from examining my own experience too closely by the tremendous demands and . . . dangers of my social situation,' he reacts by reclaiming the experience denied him. His literary reclamations of self are performances no less desperate than Wright's autobiographical tightrope between twin chronicles of growth and dissolution. But for Baldwin Wright's story, 'repeated in anger' within a first novel and then told as if newly in autobiography, must be 'told in pride,' as it already has been in black life if not black words. The pride must be national as well as racial and personal – 'Negroes are Americans and their destiny is the country's destiny.' In Baldwin as in DuBois and Wright the statement has its ironic meaning, destiny at times a doom. DuBois had asked, 'Would America have been America without her Negro people?' The answer for which the rhetorical question calls is that America will not truly *become* America without them either. Baldwin renders the prophecy in its affirmative form, however, precariously conditional as the national and personal auguries may be. If allowing himself any other position, says Baldwin at the close of 'Many Thousand Gone,' 'the Negro in America can only acquiesce in the obliteration of his own personality.' Even in *The Fire Next Time* (1963) — a slave-song resounding in Baldwin's mind a century after Emancipation — jeremiad becomes a narrative of personal effort through self-awareness to create the consciousness of others. 'Everything now, we must assume, is in our hands,' as Wright held his life in his mind, fearing fatal spillage. 'If we . . . do not falter in our duty now, we may be able . . . to end the racial nightmare, and achieve our country, and change the history of the world.'[10]

'How is it possible to write one's autobiography in a world so fast-changing as this?' asks Malcolm X, in a letter quoted by Alex Haley in his epilogue to *The Autobiography of Malcolm X* (1965). The question is one asked implicitly by Adams from first page to last of the *Education*, the outer world as ostensible subject having long since given way to demands of the inner, the autobiographical act compelled by the changes within and without which seem to prevent it. Change is for Malcolm X a matter of escalating tension between the idea of black life in America as fixed in the design imposed by slavery, and a contrary notion, inseparable from the first, of possibilities achievable through black resistance to that design. This is essentially the double-consciousness DuBois projects in *The Souls of Black Folk*, which gave Malcolm his first 'glimpse into the black people's history before they came to this country.' Under pressure of double-consciousness reminiscent of Wright, between narrowing lines of historical force, Malcolm's voice accelerates toward the end he foresees, creating in the process a self who survives before in fact destroyed. Considered in relation to the literary patterns surveyed above — of interplay between the written and the unwritten record, of the urge to articulate black self out of silence — the fact that the book was spoken to Haley is of secondary importance. *The Autobiography of Malcolm X* is what it has been called, 'a great American life, a compelling and irreplaceable book.'[11] The life violently ended (but no more violently, Malcolm argued before the fact, than the inner lives of black Americans continue to be lived) is now begun on a pilgrimage of text, which Haley makes clear is in its essence Malcolm's. The issue is finally one of readership as much as authorship, as DuBois suggested in his plea to God the Reader that his book be truly heard. As Ellison's narrator says in *Invisible Man*, the words welling in the silence after 'There's Many a Thousand Gone' is sung, 'A whole unrecorded history is spoken then, . . . listen to what is said.'

The story is told as Baldwin said it must be, compulsively, in symbols and signs, in hieroglyphics such as the cryptic notations Malcolm made on paper napkins Haley learned to leave near him during interviews. Malcolm X speaks from beyond his conversion to 'the Lost-Found Nation of Islam here in this wilderness of North America,' beyond also his break with Elijah Muhammad, a change in a 'life of changes' moving him toward a core of constant self. He speaks at times from a sense of being 'already dead,' premonitions of assassination blending with the 'whispered' rather than the documented truth of his father's lynching, with the historical fatality of his race's enslavement. Violence, as he puts it, 'runs in my family.' Such 'posthumousness' of voice, recalling moments of similar sensibility in Baldwin, Wright and DuBois, is no less emotionally convincing for being a rhetorical pose. The making of the book is on one level a political act, like Malcolm's re-enactment of his father's involvement in Marcus Garvey's 'back to Africa' movement in his own commitment to the Muslim doctrine of separation from white America. The personal progressively absorbs the political statement, however. He presents himself throughout as embodying the historical situation of 'the black man in North America' (the equivalent but also the revision of 'the Negro in America,' the phrase in which Baldwin asserted his representative role), and the psychological tension collectively experienced by blacks.

Although the *Autobiography* contains no indication that he knew *Native Son* (other than a mention of meeting Wright's widow), in several passages Malcolm *is* Bigger, holding within him the same prophecy of our future. He accepts without limiting himself to the role of 'America's most dangerous and threatening black man, . . . the one who has been kept sealed up by the Northerner in the black ghetto.' This type, like the conditions which create it, 'needs no fuse; . . . it spontaneously combusts from within.' Malcolm makes of himself the archetypal 'black prisoner,' in whose ineradicable 'memory of the bars' is also remembrance of the 'first landing of the first slave ship.' Such memory, from which historical identity has been erased, is itself the historical identity here reclaimed.

In prison, however, Malcolm also first felt free. 'Transformed' by conversion, he was also liberated into the 'new world' of books. The acts of reading and writing coalesced, as they had for Wright, into a means of self-verification against the cultural record from which he felt absent. He developed this more in terms of the spoken than the written word, his discovery of oratorical power simultaneous with the Muslims' discovery of its uses, as with narrator and Brotherhood in *Invisible Man*. But he emphasizes in the *Autobiography* his release into reading, and a consequent control of self in writing. After 'lights out,' the lamp's faint glow inversely suggesting the 1,369 bulbs blazing in Ellison's narrator's room, Malcolm feigns sleep as the guard passes, then re-enters the 'area of that light-glow' to read on. As he listens to Elijah Muhammad 'make a parable of me' while introducing him to the Muslims after he leaves prison, he is already launched on an effort to recompose himself in words.

Thus the fixity of each image of imprisonment is countered, though not negated, by a sense of fluid potentiality. Anger remains a creative force − 'I *believe* in anger,' Malcolm proclaims. He also comes to believe, however, in a different power of emergence from the past. The mental 'wings' bestowed by conversion to Islam are those he rhetorically spreads as an angel of black vengeance against the white devil. They are also the wings on which the Muslims accuse him of flying too near the sun of Elijah Muhammad's supremacy within the sect. But Malcolm X experiences the growth of other wings, within the chrysalis of personal history, to be spread in imaginative self-reincarnation.

His names, shed like snakeskin, convey the metamorphosis − Malcolm Little, 'Homeboy,' 'Detroit Red,' 'Satan,' Malcolm X, El-Hajj Malik El-Shabazz. Whole phases of inner experience slide away 'like snow off a roof,' each previous phase 'back there, without any remaining effect.' During a pilgrimage to Mecca carrying him past Black Muslim brotherhood to the true fulfillment of his Muslim life, he recalls a vision which takes him back in time as easily as the flow of time with which he is obsessed has taken him forward through his narrative. Lying awake among sleeping pilgrims,

> my mind took me back to personal memories I would have thought were gone forever, . . . as far back, even, as when I was just a little boy, eight or nine years old. Out behind our house . . . there was an old, grassy 'Hector's Hill,' we called it − which

may still be there. I remembered there in the Holy World how I used to lie on top of Hector's Hill, and look up at the sky, at the clouds moving over me, and daydreaming all kinds of things. And then . . . I remembered how years later, when I was in prison, I used to lie on my cell bunk – this would be especially when I was in solitary,[12]

his dreamings of the future unencumbered by the past, in solitary reflection his immersion in, more than his racial removal from, the world. In Mecca but in memory as well, he feels for the first time 'like a complete human being.' Prison at the time of his conversion was in Concord. He notes a link between Thoreau and himself forged in political resistance, suggesting in the process one consisting in the act of literary self-creation too. Hector's Hill, from which in the telling he reads again in moving clouds the symbols and signs of human possibility, is for a moment the imaginative place from which Thoreau would 'fish in the sky, whose bottom is pebbly with stars.'

In idiom also Malcolm slides easily through time and space, metamorphically slipping into the breaks of colloquial speech as Ellison's narrator slips into the breaks in Louis Armstrong's music, descended from the sorrow songs. He naturalizes the hustler's language into the narrative, after flaunting it at the outset, a verbal equivalent of the zoot suit he wears while inducting his Gentle Reader into the Harlem underworld. He then moves past it, as he moves beyond that phase of experience, but a fund of street intelligence remains, stenciled in his mind like the memory of the bars. As he says when he realizes that his discredit among the Muslims is being subtly arranged, 'I hadn't hustled in the streets for years for nothing. I knew when I was being set up.'

'What if history was a gambler,' wonders the narrator in *Invisible Man*. 'What if history was not a reasonable citizen, but a madman full of paranoid guile,' life thus a matter of 'running and dodging the forces of history instead of making a dominating stand.' Malcolm presents hustling as a way of life rooted in a sense similar to Ellison's, paranoid guile the only sane response to reality as the hustler perceives it. 'Internally restrained by nothing,' the hustler is also in Malcolm's term a 'gambler,' a Rinehartian being to whom anything is possible, inhabiting a world in which anything can happen. In the act of narration Malcolm's voice runs and dodges, talk from those days spilling into the present, from one form of the dangerous and reverberating silence of which Baldwin spoke. At the heart of the hustler's life is what Wright saw in his earliest stories, a 'yawning void,' an autobiographical vacuum with 'no plot, . . . nothing save atmosphere, and longing and death.' In the hustler's inability to 'appraise' his own activity, lest in such distraction he fall prey to another, is the analogue to Baldwin's sense of being prohibited by external pressure from examining his own experience, a similar loss of experience the result.

Malcolm tells of filling the void with drugs, to prolong for himself the stream of hyperactive consciousness. Cocaine, for example, makes him 'want to talk,' providing 'that feeling of timelessness . . . intervals of ability to recall and review things that had happened years back with an astonishing clarity.' In 'snow,' then, is an inverse form of the metamorphic impulse — 'snow sliding off a roof' — out of which, as autobiographer, he now speaks. The drug could reverse and compress autobiographical sequence, packing his awareness of a gambler's inevitable losses back below the surface, making of his mind an explosive charge, while seeming to create a less volatile form of autobiographical control: 'I could float [thoughts of getting caught] back where they came from until tomorrow, and then until the next day.' Bigger had similarly felt the illusion of 'destiny in his grasp' when in flight, his awareness packed down into a 'single sharp point' of concentration on his immediate survival. Malcolm also tells of the death by drugs of Billie Holiday, to him the modern interpreter of the old spirituals: 'Lady Day sang with the *soul* of Negroes from the centuries of sorrow and oppression.' He identifies her voice with his own, yet also finds retrospectively in her fate an inverse image of his own transfiguration.

Rescued in prison from the hustler's death-in-life, Malcolm found, in his role as 'the black prisoner,' the echo of the general experience of American blacks in the Muslim precept 'The white man is the devil.' Hence his susceptibility to conversion, and his insistence on the emotional truth, long after rejecting the historical absurdity, of the Muslim creation myth of 'Mr. Yacub.' Of a 'tale' told in the ghetto, about a black woman's revenge against the whites who lynched her husband, Wright wrote in *Black Boy*:

I did not know if the story was factually true or not, but it was emotionally true because I had already grown to feel that there

existed men against whom I was powerless, men who could vio-
late my life at will . . . . The story of the woman's deception
gave form and meaning to confused defensive feelings that had
long been sleeping in me.[13]

Baldwin reports in *Notes of a Native Son* a 'rumor' of a black
soldier's being shot in the back by a white policeman in Harlem's
Hotel Braddock, and dying while protecting a Negro woman from
the officer. Baldwin's correction of the facts — the soldier was
neither shot in the back nor dead, and the woman did not necessarily need protection — is secondary to the force with which the
rumor swept the streets. An 'instantaneous and revealing invention,' it gave form and meaning to confused feelings in those who
heard it: 'They preferred the invention because [it] expressed and
corroborated their hates and fears so perfectly.' In this sense, for
'that black convict' (as Malcolm calls himself) at the time of conversion, as for Malcolm having passed through self-narration
beyond such faith, 'The teachings ring true — to every Negro.'

Malcolm also mentions the incident in the Hotel Braddock, but
makes no interpretive comment, relating the 'flash' of the rumor of
the shooting without inquiring into its factuality. For him factuality is in that flash, out of which a riot spontaneously combusts.
This is an instance of the *Autobiography*'s lack of 'literary'
development of its material. The sequence is perfectly aligned,
however, with the sense of reality governing this phase of Malcolm's life. 'A writer is what I want, not an interpreter,' Haley says
Malcolm told him when the publishing contract was signed. Or, as
Ellison's narrator puts it, 'This is not prophecy, but description.'
In such description, nonetheless, is a cumulative prophecy, ignit-
ing as inevitably in Malcolm's mind as the riot explodes in Harlem.

Whatever the mix of Malcolm X's motives — outrage at a
leader's lapses from Muslim morality, perhaps the pride of a
'Satan' who would rule — in breaking and in turn being cut off
from the Muslims, he finds himself, in his final year, again on his
own. 'Thinking for myself,' running and dodging through the psychological debris of the failure for him of Muslim historical design,
he is exhilarated by freedom yet desperate for the new community
he has set out in his mind to create in this wilderness of North
America. He experiences the return — it had never really left him
— of the old double-consciousness. THEM, hieroglyphically
inscribed by Malcolm on one of Haley's napkins and meaning

The Honorable Elijah Muhammad, becomes a Pynchonesque suggestion of the justifications in reality for resumption of paranoid guile, like WASTE in *The Crying of Lot 49*.

As Malcolm begins to see in former friends the faces of those who will end his life, he feels, like Ellison's narrator and in Ellison's words, that in the Brotherhood 'was the only historically meaningful life that I could live. If I left it, I'd be nowhere,' that place of internal emptiness so often arrived at in the works discussed above. Then he begins to feel, in his own words as we learn from Haley's epilogue, but also like Ellision's narrator for whom in the novel's epilogue invisibility has become a form of strategic flexibility, that while 'I can't put my finger on exactly what my philosophy is now, . . . I'm flexible.' The statement, made in an interview not printed until after his death, reflects his having gone underground in Ellison's sense. It also reflects his posthumous determination, re-emergent in text, on lower narrative frequencies to keep on speaking for us all. This is where Malcolm X — his voice turning inward in a tightening gyre, the same tight circles he often walked while talking to Haley — makes his dominating stand.

When Malcolm lost faith in Elijah Muhammad, he felt 'as though something in *nature* had failed, like the sun, or the stars.' Elijah Muhammad, interpreting to the Muslim faithful Malcolm's fall from grace, said 'He was a star, who went astray.' Malcolm is yet another of DuBois's falling stars, dying throughout history. But he is also in his book — in which he steps into self-fulfilling imagination rather than into Rinehart's mastery of chaos — the embodiment of DuBois, and of other black American autobiographers of this century. His parents' seventh child, he is also DuBois's 'seventh son, born with a veil, and gifted with second-sight in this American world,' the gift of insight the curse of double-consciousness. Eldridge Cleaver says 'Black history began with Malcolm X,'[14] ignoring a history begun long before DuBois, yet testifying truly to the seminal as well as the culminating power of the record of Malcolm's personal journey up from slavery.

In the last lines of his *Narrative of the Life of Frederick Douglass, An American Slave, Written by Himself* (1845), Douglass states:

> The truth was, I felt myself a slave, and the idea of speaking to white people weighed me down. I spoke but a few moments, when I felt a degree of freedom, and said what I desired with

considerable ease. From that time until now, I have been engaged in pleading the cause of my brethren — with what success, and with what devotion, I leave those acquainted with my labors to decide.[15]

Malcolm's voice encompasses without overriding the voices of those who have spoken 'from that time until now.' In tones reminiscent of Douglass's he says:

I have given to this book so much of whatever time I have because I feel, and I hope, that if I honestly and fully tell my life's account, read objectively it might prove to be a testimony of some social value.[16]

He dares humbly as well as in anger and pride 'to dream to myself' — back now on Hector's Hill as well as nearing death — 'that one day, history may even say that my voice . . . helped to save America from a grave, possibly even a fatal catastrophe.' With what success remains unknown, to be revealed in cities of words as yet unbuilt in the wilderness of North America, in signs yet to appear on the open pages beneath Wright's pencil at the end of *American Hunger*. With what devotion, however, is amply answered in *The Autobiography of Malcolm X*.

Malcolm's fallen star merges with the morning star of Thoreau, his 'two-edged sword' of Islamic truth with the scimitar in *Walden*, 'the sun glimmer[ing] on both its surfaces,' its edge 'dividing you through the heart' as in *Invisible Man* the narrator hears the shattering stroke of his heart in 'There's Many a Thousand Gone.' In his parable of unfinished self, Malcolm X moves time-haunted toward the perfect work into which time does not enter, an autobiographical act in which the tale DuBois called 'twice told but seldom written' becomes one in which (in a sense other than yet comprehending that of the Islamic prophecy invoked by Malcolm) 'everything is written.'

Haley (indispensable although secondary to the process; our thanks are due him along with Malcolm's paid to Allah) speaks in his epilogue of having seen the veiled face of Malcolm X in death. But as epilogue turns prologue, he 'still can't quite conceive him dead. It still feels to me as if he has just gone into some next chapter' of experience about to be spoken into life.

'A tradition is at work here,' as Irving Howe observed in reviewing *American Hunger* with passing reference to Douglass and DuBois, aware (one assumes) of the statement's obviousness, but intent on placing Wright's posthumous volume in a context of the 'congeniality' for black writers of personal narrative as a form.[17] The making of personal memory into collective myth, and the initiation of personality through articulation of collective history, are indeed among the central, recurrent concerns of black writers in America, though it can also be argued that this tends to be true of all American literature. Whether this is to be understood as a restriction imposed on their imaginations by an audience unreceptive to their senses of themselves and their history, or as a way through such as any writer must seek — as natural as it is necessary — to full power of imagination over the world, is another question and the subject of continuing discussion.[18] The personal writings of Maya Angelou, in which blackness is less overwhelmingly than in earlier authors the focus of work cast in a variety of forms; or the stories of James Alan McPherson, which explore in *Elbow Room* for example the fictional space denied to, yet created by, Ellison's invisible man in his cramped burrow; viewed in relation to the narratives examined above, these recent efforts seem to offer evidence for both interpretations, suggesting that the truth is more complex than either.

At issue here has been instead the accumulation of a sense, within a selective representation of modern American books by black authors, of a 'tradition' in which the 'congenial' form is also resistant and problematical, doubly based as it is on both belief and unbelief in its power. This is the tradition Baldwin said would require still more words to make articulate. This is also the tradition *made* articulate by DuBois, Wright, Malcolm X and others including Baldwin. Self-separated from, as well as historically denied access to, the tradition in self-invention of Emerson, Thoreau and Whitman, they are yet directly a part of that tradition too. Each as much as Emerson finds in veiled and half-articulate symbologies of the human self the means to decipher and express the hieroglyphics of his human life. In so doing each creates the meaning of all American lives.

'One may say,' says Baldwin, 'that the Negro in America does not really exist except in the darkness of our minds,' echoing the prologue to *Invisible Man* and the paradoxical premise of the works here surveyed, sensing the spark of his being glow in the unsustaining social atmosphere of what he calls the 'darkening world.' Rather, the darkening world itself is illumined in the existence of these voices from the Veil.

4

The Cruel Radiance of What Is: James Agee

the feeling increased itself upon me that at the end of a wandering and seeking, so long it had begun before I was born, I had apprehended and now sat at rest in my own home . . .

Let Us Now Praise Famous Men

James Agee's and Walker Evans's combined narrative and photographic record of certain passages in the lives of three tenant families in rural Alabama was largely disregarded after its appearance in 1941, despite generally favorable reviews. The book's initial critics were baffled as to its intended genre, and disapproved of Agee's personal participation in the narrative. Having thus disapproved of the work's raison d'être, however − its documentary value being utterly inseparable from its author's self-investment in the subject − these critics praised the volume, in terms conditioned by their uncertainty as to how to classify it, for the 'honesty' and 'originality' of its prose.[1] Declining interest in the system of Southern sharecropping as an object of reformist activity, compounded by Agee's assault within the text on reigning documentary expectations and reformist pieties, caused *Let Us Now Praise Famous Men* to go unread, by an American public increasingly preoccupied by the spread of world war.

Since publication of the second edition in 1960, five years after Agee's death, *Let Us Now Praise Famous Men* has been widely read and generally acclaimed as 'classic,' but in terms which continue to reflect the critical uncertainties of 1941. Agee's personal presence in the narrative is now as often grounds for praise as for blame. His attack on documentary conventions of the time now seems less outrageous than he clearly meant it to be then. But the work remains uncertainly understood as to genre, uneasily discussed as to the system or lack thereof in its narrative procedures and mixtures of formal elements. A reviewer of the first edition found in it 'the proportions of a major novel,'[2] seeking in his confusion over what it actually *was* some clarifying sense of what it might instead (and to more recognizably 'major' effect) have *been*. More recent readers have also sought to define the book by relocating their impressions of its shape and significance within more familiar contexts, such as that suggested by 'novel.' Agee himself perhaps invited this sort of response by offering analogies between his text and film or music, or indeed by suggesting correspondences with fiction. He called his narrative 'a *book* only by necessity.' Its particular necessities of form and feeling, however — its inevitabilities *as* a book which accumulates from within rather than conforms to surrounding molds of analogy to established modes — have tended as a result to be difficult to define.

Let Us Now Praise Famous Men is, as Alfred Kazin called it in *On Native Grounds*, a 'documentary book written to end all documentary books.'[3] (Agee called it in his preface a deliberate 'insult, and a corrective' to standard documentary methods of the 1930s.) It is also, as William Stott terms it in *Documentary Expression and Thirties America*, a 'classic . . . because it culminates the central rhetoric of the time, and explodes it, surpasses it.'[4] The book having culminated the central rhetoric of its time and violently broken the generic mold in which it was initially cast, however, the question of what remains amid the fragments of a shattered form — of what the book may be said to have *become*, and from what sources of alternative rhetoric within itself — continues to be both centrally interesting and incompletely known.

Agee's text, rather than the photographs by Evans which comprise an integral part of *Let Us Now Praise Famous Men*, is at issue here, 'coequal' as Agee called Evans's images with his own, and useful as Evans's insights into the narrative have since proved. It is taken for granted rather than disputed that photographs and text are in some sense (as Agee put it) 'mutually independent and fully collaborative.' It is also assumed, however, that what binds Agee's book into the structure of this study is the problem not of relationship between words and photographic images, but rather of relationship between what Agee calls his 'nominal' and his 'actual' subjects:

> The nominal subject is North American cotton tenantry as examined in the daily living of three representative white tenant families.
>
> Actually, the effort is to recognize the stature of a portion of unimagined existence, and to contrive techniques proper to its recording, communication, analysis, and defense. More essentially, this is an independent inquiry into certain normal predicaments of human divinity.
>
> The immediate instruments are two: the motionless camera, and the printed word. The governing subject — is individual, anti-authoritative human consciousness.
>
> Ultimately, it is intended that this record and analysis be exhaustive, with no detail, however trivial it may seem, left untouched, no relevancy avoided, which lies within the power of remembrance to maintain, of the intelligence to perceive, and of the spirit to persist in.
>
> Of this ultimate intention the present volume is merely portent and fragment, experiment, dissonant prologue.[5]

Agee's declaration of purpose both uncoils and ascends in an Emersonian spiral, from 'nominal' through 'actual' and 'more essential' toward 'ultimate' intention, which then recollapses into a sense of the process as 'mere portent' of the truth he would tell. In so doing it prefigures, more than it really describes or explains, the characteristic rhythm of the book as a whole.

The tenant families are of 'nominal' interest in that they are the means to Agee's ends as a 'swindler' of standard documentary expectations, a 'spy' along with Evans behind the lines of 'enemy' reportorial technique. They are in this sense as incidental to the issue as a civilian population is 'defenseless' (so Agee often terms the tenants) against the ebb and flow of warfare in which victory and defeat abstractly assessed in terms of territorial gain and loss. More importantly, however, the families are 'nominal' in that their very representativeness of a general socio-economic subject requires their 'actualization' as unique human beings. They need in Agee's view to be 'named' in order to be brought into full being, to be redeemed from unimagined existence, and in order for the reality of that existence to be made inescapably apparent to all.

Thus 'Woods,' 'Gudger' and 'Rickets' are not only pseudonyms for Fields, Burroughs and Tingle,[6] strategically appropriate to the journalistic task at hand even if undercut by the photographs' disclosure (to those who would recognize them) of particular identities. Woods, Gudger and Ricketts are also 'true' names, in a sense transcending the conventions of confidentiality, of 'characters' in a drama of what Agee calls human divinity. The governing narrative principle (not merely the instrument) of this dramatization is Agee's own encompassing (not simply observing) consciousness, itself the center as well as the surrounding medium of the subject.

On the one hand Agee argues that the eye of Evans's camera records a reality that requires no elaboration. On the other hand Agee's text, several-hundred-page portent of what he originally projected as requiring hundreds more, is from first to last an elaboration of the idea that to recognize the reality of his subjects' lives is necessarily to inquire into the reality of his own. The first person singular, carefully eliminated from the statement of purpose quoted above however obvious between the lines, explicitly emerges as the book's basic point of ontological as well as grammatical reference, in a passage in which — disclaiming art — Agee redefines his problem in terms of narrative enactment of himself:

> In a novel, a house or person has his meaning, his existence, entirely through the writer. Here, a house or a person has only the most limited of his meaning through me: his true meaning is much huger. It is that he *exists*, in actual being, as you do and as I do, and as no character of the imagination can possibly exist. His great weight, mystery and dignity are in this fact. As for me, I can tell you of him only what I saw, only so accurately as in my terms I know how: and this in turn has its chief stature not in any ability of mine but in the fact that I too exist, not as a work of fiction, but as a human being.[7]

To be, he goes on to say — to share with his subjects at the moment of communion with them the 'immeasurable weight [of] actual existence' — is to write, to 'tell,' with a power he differentiates from that of the novelist, but for which he claims an equivalent capacity to reconstruct the world.

Not as a work of fiction, then, but through a form of self-artistry nonetheless, to tell the tenants' story is to enter his own mind, a 'universe luminous, spacious, incalculably rich and wonderful in each detail, as relaxed and natural to the human swimmer, and as full of glory, as his breathing.' Stott says of Evans that in his pictures of the tenants he 'suggests that all they touch and all that touches them, is permeated with their being. Whereas the prosperous attenuate their selfhood through many possessions and roles, the poor condense theirs in a few. Their world and everything in it bespeaks them, symbolizes them. It is entirely a work of art.'[8] Attenuating himself into their world in an effort to achieve the verbal equivalent of Evans's images, then collapsing those images into the cosmos of his own consciousness, Agee appropriates the tenants' world and permeates it with his being. He does so to repossess them of it, to make of the sheer fact of their existence what Joan Didion would later call an 'idea in the world's mind' true to his personal sense of the mystery and dignity of their lives. But running still deeper is a drive on Agee's part to make their lives bespeak and symbolize *his*, to condense himself into the conditions of their existence and so actualize himself along with them.

This too would of course also be 'entirely a work of art.' Agee's disavowal of authorial responsibility for the 'meaning' of the tenants' story thus resembles, and also arrives at the underlying self-assertion of, Emerson's 'I am nothing; I see all,' the act of seeing in turn for both the supremely active form of being. Such seeming self-negation constitutes a claim to control over the world thus envisioned which is present in Agee's every denial of shaping influence on his material. Each of his confessions of inadequacy to the task, a task to which throughout the book he reconsiders and recommences his approach, contains without contradicting his sense of seeking to master his subject by becoming coterminous with it. The narrative 'a *book* only by necessity,' in the negative sense of the limitations of print, Agee as protagonist of necessity becomes the book, in the imperially positive sense of Whitman's edict in *Leaves of Grass*, 'Who touches this touches a man.'

The presumption involved in setting out (no matter how often he also damns the intention) to make 'real' the lives of others is truly monstrous. The literary-technical *hubris* involved in seeking (no matter how fiercely he also rejects the claims of art) to contrive techniques capable of transcending their own limitations is unfulfillably vast, notwithstanding that art might be said to consist precisely in the effect's transcendence of the means by which it is achieved. Within rather than in opposition to Agee's urge to such overreachings, however, pulses his determination first to project, and finally to merge with, a persona in whom the tenants' unimagined lives are both honored and imaginatively fulfilled. These constant pulsations toward personal as well as literary form establish the rhythm which in its very randomness and lack of any other than momentary resolution comes to be the work's organizing principle. If, as Stott notes, disorderliness '*is* the order in the text,' so too the personal quest − like that of DuBois or Wright or Baldwin in the previous chapter − finds its own fulfillment in the intensity rather than the completion of the search for self.

The narrative pressures of his self-consciousness would ideally be commensurate with the pressures under which the identities of the tenants are condensed into their surroundings. In its inward reach his self-consciousness would also aspire to be commensurate with, and therefore to encompass, the contours of the continent. Alabama is America, particularly at night when, borne in on itself by darkness yet made luminous and infinitely spacious (as Agee described the universe of consciousness) by starlight, the region 'dreams,' becoming a land 'which exists only in the imagination and somewhere in the past.' It is mapped in the American literary past, witness Agee's suggestion of convergences in imaginative topography between his work and that of various writers extending from Faulkner back to Mark Twain. Its shape is also etched in the sound of 'the broken heart of Louis Armstrong,' as later for Ellison in the prologue to *Invisible Man*, and earlier for some who had already sought the future of the nation in the sorrow songs of those denied by the nation in the past. This America continues to be mapped, however, in the tracings of a narrative line into each personal moment of which Agee struggles to incorporate a sense of American time and space. In the 'darkness of the peopled room that is chambered in the darkness of the continent before the unwatching stars,' he listens as life resolves itself into the breathing of the sleeping Gudgers. Breathing is the analogue to his idea of the 'swimmer's' natural movement in the currents of consciousness. In a similar silence of the mind, Agee hopes to make 'the whole of that landscape we shall essay to travel in . . . visible' in prose, to ensure that 'its living map may not be neglected, however lost the breadth of the country may be in the winding walk of each sentence.'

A paradigmatic instance of Agee's method occurs early in the text, when in 'A Country Letter' he positions himself alone at a table in the Gudger house, looking at the flame of a coal-oil lamp. It is late at night ('Night was his time,' says Evans in a foreword), he is occasionally writing while everyone else in the house is sleeping, 'but just now, I am entirely focused on the lamp, and light.' The world is for the moment drawn into and annihilated by the circle of lamplight, and the flame — 'like a thought, a dream, the future' — unites through Agee's concentration on the mechanism of the lamp his mental process, his prose, the members of the Gudger household and the mysteries of the physical universe, recurrently embodied in the 'metal fire' of the stars. His sense of seasonal as well as diurnal time suspended in 'the held breath, of a planet's year,' the summer night becomes for him, along with the Gudgers plunged in sleep, a 'shared withdrawal to source,' from which the narrative as well as the human reconstitutions of daily living must spring: 'And it is in these terms I would tell you, at all leisure and in all detail, whatever there is to tell: of where I am; of what I perceive.'

As (Agee says elsewhere) 'surrounding objects are masked by looking into a light,' here 'this mere fact of thinking' holds the world at a distance, yet circumscribes a lamplit world within which, 'while my eyes are on this writing,' reality is reconstructed. All over Alabama the lamps are out, and people are drawn together in shelters as tenuous as the 'carapace' of Agee's consciousness. Within these enclosures the timeless 'composition' of the human family — which he delineates in receding generational perspective — becomes an act of personal genealogy. He contracts himself along with his subjects, huddled in the night against the 'enormous assaults of the universe,' into a question — 'do we really exist at all?' — the answer to which then takes shape as an affirmation of the Gudgers' lives in terms of his own presence at the 'magnetic center' of their family:

> and I become not my own shape and weight and self, but that of each of them, the whole of it, sunken in sleep like stones; so that I know almost the dreams they will not remember, and the soul and body of each of these seven, and of all of them together in this room in sleep, as if they were music I were hearing.[9]

'Foundered' in sleep (the image of home as a ship imperiled on a sea of indifferent starlight recurs), the family is also founded anew by an act of autobiographical appropriation, in which Agee claims the power to transcribe into narrative the 'music' of his life immersed in theirs.

He is here at the height of his own sense of this power. At times he is vampiristic in the intensity of his desire to suffuse himself into, and define himself in terms of, another's being, as when he yearns to 'section and lift away a part of this so thin shell' of the sleeping Emma's skull, and enter her brain. More often throughout the sequence, his story pulses out into more concretely descriptive treatment of the family's daylight routines, from the lamplit center of his nocturnal meditations. Now too, however, Agee's personal past often surfaces within and directs his handling of such descriptions. He recalls having 'as a child in the innocence of faith [had] to bring myself out of bed through the cold lucid water of the Cumberland morning and to serve at the altar at earliest lonely Mass, whose words were thrilling brooks of music and whose motions, a grave dance.' The recollection informs his near-liturgical recitation of the 'gestures,' no less beautiful or grave, with which the Gudgers' day begins. In sacramental silence, 'masked with the chill of the water that holds them together' in ritual cleansing (and that bonds these matins to Agee's Cumberland morning), they kindle a fire and prepare their food. The scene then expands to include the Woods and Ricketts families, the ceremonies for each 'much the same,' 'a little different,' after which the inhabitants of all three houses are 'scattered on the wind of a day's work,' as the narrative has scattered from the source to which it had withdrawn.

The episode spreads textually driven by Agee's presumption to power, drawn from the personal source, to 'tell you anything . . . that I wish to tell you, and . . . what so ever it may be, you will not be able to help but understand it.' The process is seeded throughout, however, with moments in which that confidence is undercut by a sense of inability to tell truly, or to be fully understood. A portion of the sequence deals with Agee's sexual feeling for Emma, and his assumption, for which he offers only subjective evidence, of reciprocal feeling on her part. The subject occasions a shift in chronology his apparent control of which seems qualified by excessive explanation, at a point in the book by which the reader has followed Agee through several such maneuvers: 'But here I am going to shift ahead of where I am writing, to a thing which is to happen . . . (you mustn't be puzzled by this, I'm writing in a continuum)'. The subject is also one of the occasions for the frankness

Agee flaunts as one of the sources of the book's necessary violence against conventional proprieties. Yet the situation diffuses into language which, in striving to realize the fantasy as fact, emphasizes in the end Agee's failure to complete the imaginative act: 'I can swear that I now as then almost believe that in that moment she would have so well understood this, . . . but instead . . . .' Emma's departure from the Gudger house — the imminence of which in narrative sequence prompted Agee to probe his feelings in a narrative 'shift ahead' — is then related. She disappears down a road, 'and that,' says Agee of her fading from view, suggesting that the very effort to tell all this has somehow lost her to his inner eye, 'is Emma.'

The merits of the scene, in terms of literary strategy or of Agee's entitlement to the feelings he imputes to Emma, are less to the point here than the fact that the scene consumes itself. 'I can tell you anything' devolves into 'What's the use trying to say what I felt.' So too 'A Country Letter' as a whole, each section of which pulses toward full articulation before receding into a sense of things unsayable or left unsaid, subsides into acceptance of incompletion, indeed asserts it as a 'profounder kind of communication.' As they prepare for sleep, the Gudgers' talk sinks toward silence, words like wellwater flowing slowly and sporadically after pumping has ceased. It is a 'rhythm to be completed by answer and made whole by silence, a lyric song, as horses who nudge one another in pasture.' It is also, as Agee concludes on a note of seemingly endless morning — so had DuBois and before him Thoreau — the song of a black mule-driver who lifts 'joyfully, three times into the emblazoned morning the long black sorrow-foundered and incompleted phrase of an archaic mode in whose glorying he begins each day.' And virtually on the next page, at the outset of the sequence Agee names 'Colon' (which would seem paradoxically to exhaust that punctuation mark's suggestion of narrative inexhaustibility), the cycle begins anew: 'But there must be an end to this; . . . a new and more succinct beginning' yet another withdrawal to narrative source, in Agee's self-projection from the lamplight of his imagination.

Let Us Now Praise Famous Men repeats this pattern throughout. Agee's sense of what 'I can do' as a writer in relation to his subject coalesces with a sense of what 'I am,' his sense of *in*ability to 'tell' truly of the tenants (to say nothing of actually meliorating their condition) culminates periodically in a sense of 'who the hell am I, who in Jesus' name am I.' His ambivalence toward techniques of literary art, some of which he knows he needs, and his aspiration combined with resistance to the name of 'artist' in pursuit of this project, remain crucial to his sense of literary-technical predicament, in which the same cycles of personal advance and retreat are apparent. The example of Joyce is put to correspondingly ambiguous use: 'It took a great artist seven years to record nineteen hours and to wring them anywhere near dry. Figure it out for yourself; this lasted several weeks, not nineteen hours,' which suggests by false logic that Agee's book is therefore a more ambitious undertaking than *Ulysses*, yet which acknowledges the totality of Joyce's commitment as the ideal, even as Agee disclaims it as a model. Increasingly the problem of literary procedure becomes an aspect of the 'nominal' subject, in proliferating discussion of its irresolution Agee's only means of moving toward its solution, to which he ironically seems closest in those moments when he relaxes into acceptance of its insolubility. The vocabulary of literary procedure, shot through with Agee's version of the vocabulary of photographic procedure, also increasingly becomes a metaphorical system (notwithstanding his recurrent self-exhortation to 'abjure all metaphor') of reference to his pilgrim's progress as author-protagonist.

'George Gudger is a man,' he states for example with deliberately uncharacteristic brevity in '(On the Porch: 2':

> But obviously, in the effort to tell of him (by example) as truthfully as I can, I am limited. I know him only so far as I know him, and only in those terms in which I know him; and all of that depends as fully on who I am as on who he is.
>
>   I am confident of being able to get at a certain form of the truth about him, *only* if I am as faithful as possible to Gudger as I know him, to Gudger as, in his actual flesh and life (but there again always in my mind's and memory's eye) he is. But of course it will be only a relative truth.[10]

Repetitious, even tautological, the statement in itself represents no advance whatsoever in methodological certainty over the passage quoted earlier, from the first pages of 'Book Two' written in amplification of the 'Preface,' and ending in 'I too exist, not as a work of fiction, but as a human being.' Indeed, the earlier passage is on its surface more self-assured than this, as to the difference between 'fictional' and 'actual' being, and as to the absolute superiority of the latter form of truth. Here, in his relative lack of such assurance, however, Agee asserts 'relative truth' as being the greater as well as the lesser form of reality. One thinks of the final line in Frost's 'The Most of It,' in which the phrase, 'and that was all,' in its very ambiguity makes a similar claim for the sufficiency of a limited vision.

Agee *has* here arrived, from the earlier statement, at a degree of aesthetic control over the paradoxes his enhanced recognition of which animates and makes strategically maneuverable his persona. He withdraws into paradox as into lamplight, in his '(but there again always in my mind's and memory's eye)' the same conversion of negative into positive position *vis-à-vis* the world which Ellison's invisible man achieves in recognizing that always, even underground, 'there's the mind, the *mind*.' He compacts 'I' into 'he' (Gudger) and 'you' (the reader), actual distinctions among the three becoming ostensible as he circles in on himself, then vanishing completely as his voice joins with those who (as he puts it in a note on night as a medium of narrative) 'talk of themselves to themselves in silence.' He accepts and enacts, even as he resists, an idea of himself as fictionalizer and *hence* actualizer of 'certain shapes of fact,' a 'certain form of the truth,' which are as revealing of the essence of his own life as (by example) Gudger's. As such he molds the flux of his material back outward, having first drawn it inward, toward 'the proportions of a major novel' his reviewer, not without insight after all in his bewilderment, had discerned. Agee has something of Ishmael's capacity to make self-designation ('Call me . . .') resound throughout, yet to make the same imperative the mere − and perhaps hypothetical, or 'fictional' − pretext for his functioning as the medium of, rather than the main actor in, the narrative. In this case *along* with Gudger, or rather with a 'Gudger' once *further* removed from the Burroughs for whom George Gudger stands, Agee works to show 'how each is [himself]; and how each is a shapener' of the other. Be he agent or be he principal, as Melville has Ahab speculate of the whale in a sense not entirely unrelated to the generation of narrative, Agee is Ahab to the hooded phantom (as Ishmael thinks of Moby-Dick) of his own consciousness. So too he calls the newborn's arrival from 'the blind bottom of the human sea' a voyage ending (as does Ishmael's) as much as beginning in self-confrontation, a human child doomed as well as destined in living out the human story 'to find himself.'

Stott terms '(On the Porch: 2' the 'intellectual center' of *Let Us Now Praise Famous Men*. It is indeed a sequence in which the narrative's lines of force might most forcibly intersect, transfixing Agee as governing instrument and also as one of the centers of the subject, just as he seeks throughout to locate the heart of the human realities he observes, transfixed in cosmic darkness by 'the stars' trillions of javelins.' *Let Us Now Praise Famous Men* as importantly, however, approaches its imaginative end in '(On the Porch: 2,' which leads directly (notwithstanding that intervening material is transected) into the lyric song of Agee's brief concluding section, '(On the Porch: 3.' As the word 'orphan' at the end of *Moby-Dick* requires the act of self-naming with which that book begins; as epilogue turns prologue in *The Autobiography of Malcolm X*; so Agee, the last sentence at his book's 'intellectual center' repeated at the outset of its imaginative closure, regathers within his 'I' the elements of identity from which the narrative as a whole has flowed.

He is effortlessly together now with Evans, having struggled visibly throughout to fuse 'I' with camera eye, to shift consciousness 'from the imagined, the revisive, to . . . the cruel radiance of what is.' Yet the 'we' in which he incorporates Evans − textual embodiment of the 'Jimmy 'n' Walker' of whom members of the tenant families would later speak with affection mixed with bitterness over confidence betrayed and imagined profits unshared[11] − is as thorough an act of imaginative appropriation as any in the volume. It encompasses also the families with whom they lived for a time, and the reader, 'no less centrally involved than the authors and those of whom they tell.' Having broken 'the paralysis of [literal] parentage' (again the example of Joyce, active if unclaimed), having borne (if only in imagination, fully aware of the difference) the crushing family inheritance of tenant work, Agee moves in a medium of self-generation, for all that here, as elsewhere in the book, the transcendent moment passes and the persona once more subsides. If given to such concision, Agee instead of Oscar Wilde might have said that one's true life is the one which one doesn't really lead. Instead, in the Gudger home, he finds his narrative 'life,' the autobiographical chapters of his experience with his 'subjects,' fulfilled in a moment of self-possession felt as self-loss:

> all that surrounded me, that silently strove in through my senses
> and stretched me full, was familiar and dear to me as nothing

else on earth, and as if well known in a deep past and long years lost; so that I could wish all my chance life was in truth the betrayal, the curable delusion, that it seemed, and that this was my right home, right earth, right blood, to which I would never have true right.[12]

As the Gudgers' voices lapsed into silence at bedtime in 'A Country Letter,' so Agee's sinks in '(On the Porch: 3,' wellwater words commingling with the world, retroactively merging the narrative process with 'the operations of water among whose spider lacings by chance we live.'

Agee and Evans listen on the porch at night to 'a sound that was new to us,' the call completed by answer and made whole by silence of foxes, 'if they were foxes.' This calling, in 'mutual listening' to which the listeners are immersed in the darkness so often for Agee the agent of his self-formulations, becomes another figure for the work's overall process. Human observers and the people observed, like the unseen animal voices, 'gave each other more and more value, like the exchanges of two mirrors laid face to face.' The image's suggestion of a narcissistic symbiosis, like the solipsism of the human figure in Frost's 'The Most of It,' is transcended in the continuing application. This sound, like the human facts 'nominally' inherent in North American cotton tenantry (Alabama both echo and portent of Malcolm X's, and his forerunners', wilderness of North America), 'is one of a universe of things which should be accepted and recorded for its own sake.'

As if shifting between 'different techniques or mediums,' says Agee of his effort to record an impression of one of the Gudgers' rooms, in the method embraced still a shadow of the method abandoned, 'what began as "rembrandt," deeplighted in gold, in each integer colossally heavily planted, has become a photograph, a record in clean, staring, colorless light, almost without shadow,' the mental equivalent of an Evans print. So also with the animals' song. As Agee says elsewhere, 'the music of what is happening is more richly scored than this; and much beyond what I can set down.' This music nonetheless 'repeated itself on the ear's memory silently yet keenly as print,' a printed text in which different techniques or mediums conspire in personal narrative toward a certain form of the truth.

5

The Word for Mirror: Mary McCarthy

and I remember we heard a nightingale together, on the boulevard, near the Sacred Heart convent. But there are no nightingales in North America.

Memories of a Catholic Girlhood

The closing section of Mary McCarthy's *Memories of a Catholic Girlhood* is called 'Ask Me No Questions,' and the reader clearly hears as if in echo, even sees in the white space between title and text, 'and I'll Tell You No Lies.' Throughout the essays making up *Memories* – most published in magazines between 1946 and 1957, then revised and collected in 1957 with interchapters reflecting on the process of their composition – she has asked herself questions, reconstructing herself (as Henry James, 'removed from Family,' had in *The American Scene*) in relation to family history. The answers, or rather her meditations on the questions, while far from 'lies' and indeed for her the nearest thing to 'truth,' make problems of relation between factual and fictional narrative central to the accumulated volume. 'Many a time,' she states, 'in the course of doing these memoirs, I have wished that I were writing fiction. The temptation to invent has been very strong, particularly where recollection is hazy and I remember the substance of an event but not the details – the color of a dress, the pattern of a carpet, the placing of a picture,'[1] precisely the sorts of details which in her fiction, as in James's, can obliquely convey a human truth. The figure in the carpet, however – the missing key – becomes in her reformulation of 'these memories of mine' a figure for a mental space within which both autobiographer and novelist conspire more than they contend. To fill this space, projected as an unwritten page, with consciousness of the search for defining relation between personal past and present, becomes a purpose in which question and answer, mystery and solution, fact and invention, are fused.

Having initially put the case in terms of sharp distinction between 'memory' and 'story' — she expresses surprise that some readers of the magazine versions took them for fiction, and says 'to me, this record lays a claim to being historical' — she nonetheless pursues the case in terms of the inevitable 'storytelling' involved in the act of memory. Memory can stubbornly resist 'the stubborn facts on record.' It can also, however, be brought into being by facts which dissolve into, rather than resist, a fictive (though not necessarily inaccurate) construct of recollection: 'Now that I have established this, or nearly established it, I have the feeling of "remembering," as if I had always known it.' Like James thrilling to the 'nightingale' effect of unanticipated aesthetic satisfaction in *The American Scene*'s 'Arcadian' sequence, subsuming in his comment that bird's absence from America, McCarthy leaves stubbornly opposed to this fact of natural history her 'memory' of hearing a nightingale with her father in Seattle. 'Mendacity, somewhere, in the McCarthy blood,' is finally less the paternal taint in the background of her own verbal negotiations with the truth (still less the familial miasma of self-deception pervading Tennessee Williams's *Cat on a Hot Tin Roof*) than a kind of creativity for which her occasional apologies never quite ring true.

She also turns the 'great handicap to this task of recalling,' the fact of being an orphan, into a paradigm of incentive to the literary task. The chain of her family's 'collective memory' broken by her parents' death in a flu epidemic when she was six, she feels herself 'reduced . . . chiefly to my own memory,' her remaining relatives (excepting her brother Kevin) described as disinclined to discuss the past. (Henry Adams had by contrast found a point of departure in a pose as one rendered personally superfluous by the overpowering collective memory of an historically self-conscious family.) Such 'reduction' to personal recall, however, is the narrative circumstance she recurrently seeks, an intensification more than an impoverishment of self. The 'quest' she says she and her brother still pursue, drawing relatives by their own marriages into 'archaeological' conjecture as to the meanings inferable from fragmentary evidence, is concentrated in the text more purely within her own persona, as one for whom 'the very difficulties in the way have provided an incentive' to self-conjecture. 'When I say "we," however, perhaps I mean only myself . . . .' She speaks of the 'aesthetic' shock involved in the loss of her parents, referring to her six-year-old's sense of a shift in style and taste occasioned by her placement with relatives in Minneapolis. In a more strictly literary sense, the adult's perspective reabsorbing the child's, she makes of the shock (in all its aspects) of being orphaned a problem in which the aesthetics of self-portraiture merge with matters of moral judgment or historical verification. 'Home' becomes − in the present narrative endeavor as well as in the recollected past − the architecture of personality.

The church initially provided the 'aesthetic outlet' she required, in its verbal as much as its physical forms 'the equivalent of Gothic cathedrals,' a referent of personal aspiration and orderly progress toward goals. So Adams had found in such structures the equivalent of an ideal of unified cultural aspiration, against which cultural movement, as experienced in personal consciousness, into twentieth-century multiplicity might be measured. McCarthy re-envisions 'the words of the Mass and the Litanies and the old Latin hymns' as a framework of the mind surrounding an interior space within which to 'dream' a self. In this context she presents an incident archetypically significant to her, as containing the 'pattern' of her subsequent experience. Having inadvertently taken water and thus broken her fast while preparing for her first Communion, she agonizes over what she feels would be the moral fatality of commencing her religious life in a state of sin, knowing also that she will not forego the occasion. Aware in retrospect on the one hand of the child's exaggerated sense of the lapse, she also affirms the adult's 'dry self-knowledge' of her own insoluble 'conflict between excited scruples and inertia of will.' The persona's 'damnation' in the narrative present, for the child's transgression in the reimagined past, consists in the constant re-enactment of that conflict. Yet she also finds in such re-enactment an emblem of salvation, with its own implications for the act of literary survival now being attempted in autobiography, as well as for her survival then of supposedly mortal crisis of the soul.

Seemingly offered in impartial explanation, rather than in self-extenuation, the 'unconscious resistance' brought on in the child by excitement but also perhaps by the taboo itself, becomes for the adult a resource through which to engage the world. Having already dramatized a struggle with conscience suggestive of Huckleberry Finn's ('It was a close place'), she alludes to (without naming, perhaps because the name is absurdly apt) the 'heroine of one of my novels,' Martha Sinnott in *A Charmed Life*. Martha's pregnancy, possibly the consequence of an infidelity of which her husband is unaware, constitutes 'the same fix, morally,' as that of the new Communicant. Martha dies in an automobile accident, a 'fatal mistake' distinct from yet also reflective of the insolubility of her dilemma of acknowledgment. Just before the crash, however (singing words from one of the old Latin hymns), she suddenly knows 'without knowing how she knew' that she could 'trust herself' whatever her decision: 'She had changed; she was no longer afraid of herself. That was the reward of that fearsome decision which no longer seemed fearsome, now that it was behind her.'[2]

As in *Memories*, authorial irony is present but is also transcended in the character's affirmation of a personal 'resistance' centered deep within, against definition of herself by others or according to institutional forms. In Martha's Latin song, as in McCarthy's sense in *Memories* (like DuBois's in *The Souls of Black Folk*) of an old song's shaping power in the present, is something of the act of self-salvation in Huck's 'All right, then, I'll *go* to hell.' Dry self-knowledge — with its suggestion of Gerontion's 'After such knowledge, what forgiveness?' — becomes in McCarthy's development of the Communion sequence a source of fluid self-inquiry in continuing narrative, forward motion more than forgiveness the issue. (Gerontion's sensibility seems much like Adams's, even if Eliot may have misconstrued Adams in terms of himself, and though McCarthy's absorption of the line from Eliot's poem seems finally more consistent with the operation of the Adams persona.) Moreover, she further reinforces a notion of the episode's significance as lying more in the narrational than in the moral outcome, by citing — as if to verify her own 'story' by literary analogue — a 'story almost identical with mine' told her by Ignazio Silone.

McCarthy accords Latin literature, and history as taught in parochial school, a similarly salutary influence on her 'character,' in a sense ultimately emphasizing self-fictionalization over moral development; or perhaps the telling of a 'story' of one's life as the pertinent *form* of moral development. Catholic bias in historical interpretation, or the 'partisanships' of the Latin authors, call forth the same internal 'resistance,' less in the sense of revolt against doctrine than in that of the capacity to exert historical consciousness as personal force. 'To care for the quarrels of the past, to identify oneself passionately with a cause that became, politically speaking, a losing cause with the birth of the modern world, is to experience a kind of straining against the reality.' The point is not that she is therefore embattled against the modern world, any more than that as a lapsed Catholic she has lost the systems of religious metaphor through which she continues to express herself. It is rather that in 'straining against reality' one defines oneself in relation to reality. (Joan Didion, as discussed in a chapter to follow, makes a similar claim for 'adverse' relation to reality as a form of full engagement with it.) McCarthy's claim is not to the narrative freedom to reconstruct (or like Samuel Clemens's Satan in *The Mysterious Stranger* to deconstruct) the world in its entirety in personal consciousness. She claims rather to have shaped − in the act of literary remembrance as well as in the actual experience she recalls − a persona able, like the heroine of *A Charmed Life* and perhaps her other novels as well, to trust more than to fear herself. Through this persona she seeks to fill from within the spaces carved by the mind's 'fictions,' or left empty by the inaccessibility of 'fact,' in the still-resistant actuality of the world without.

The 'pattern' of the first Communion repeats itself incrementally throughout the book, most notably in McCarthy's 'theft' of the tin butterfly, her 'decision' to lose her faith, the 'discovery' of her menstrual cycle, and her shift in self-imagining allegiance from Catiline to him 'who wrote not "I" but "Caesar."' The 'fact' of Uncle Myers having planted the missing butterfly, causing McCarthy to be blamed and then whipping her for the theft, dissolves without being definitely contradicted in the interchapter's 'awful suspicion' that her drama teacher later suggested that interpretation for a play, never finished, McCarthy attempted in school. (One thinks for a moment of James's difficulties as a dramatist, and those qualities of inwardly ruminative mind, more than any of syntax as such, which in McCarthy's work as well might tend to resist the compressions of playwriting.) But in 'fusing two memories' − an act her '*mea culpa*' seems to affirm rather than deny − she completes the previously unfinished literary act. She also confirms in the interchapter the original essay's emphasis on her sense of 'inner victory,' a heroine's resistant identity the central 'fact' of the matter, rather than the unanswerable 'But who did put the butterfly by my place?' So too McCarthy's strategic profession of loss of faith, so that the convent would 'know *who I was*,' prompts the deeper discovery that belief had already been displaced into metaphor, on which she could nonetheless in some ways still rely, the fearsome decision like Martha Sinnott's no longer fearsome because behind her.

Playing Catiline in her school's Latin Club play, 'Marcus Tullius,' McCarthy awaits her cue as Cicero orates, lounging 'with a scornful smile on my dark, ruined features':

> From my lonely bench, I surveyed them in superb isolation, the damned soul, proud and unassimilable, the marked, gifted man. I paused, as though hesitating to waste my words on these gentry, and then leapt to my feet and delivered Catiline's speech, *in toto*, as recorded by Sallust — a short tirade, unfortunately, highly colored but stiff, ending in the *défi* 'I will extinguish the flames of my own ruin in the conflagration of all Rome.' Now this speech, from the start, had bothered me. With its threats and bombast, its Senecan frigidity, it sounded guilty and rather stupid. Even making allowances for Sallust's prejudice . . . , the effect of repeating it night after night in rehearsal had awakened a tiny doubt: Was the Catiline I admired so much merely a vulgar arsonist, as Cicero and his devotees contended? These first stirrings of maturity were very unwelcome. To my mind, Catiline was not only a hero — he was me.[3]

As before in *Memories*, for example in connection with 'inner victory' in 'The Tin Butterfly' or the effort to make her schoolmates know *'who I was'* in 'C'est le Premier Pas Qui Coûte,' self-deprecatory irony modulates more than it obliterates McCarthy's sense of herself as the heroine of a fundamentally serious narrative drama, with issues of personal identity genuinely at stake. 'It did not, of course, occur to me that there was also "another" me, behind the Catilinarian poses,' that in preparing for the production of the play, with none of the ironic detachment which is part of the recollecting persona's pose, she was coming also to see certain other 'strange landscapes in myself.'

The discovery of Caesar, an author-protagonist in his *Commentaries* in a sense, McCarthy suggests, not wholly different from that in which she compiles her *Memories*, is therefore at once disturbing and preordained in its effect. All her previous acts of identification with literary, legendary or historical figures 'had been products of my will, constructs of my personal convention, or projections of myself, the way Catiline was. This came from without and seized me.' She writes of the experience, more archly than ironically, in terms of defloration: 'nothing . . . could have warned me that Caesar would be like *this*'; 'it might have happened with another − with Thucydides, say, if Greek had been offered.' But in also calling it her 'first piercing contact with an impersonal reality,' she moves beneath this tonal veneer, re-entering more than lightly mocking her situation as she felt it then. Caesar is to her (the 'very grammar was beatified for me by the objective temperament that ordered it') 'just, laconic, severe, magnanimous, detached.' But she responds as well to a 'mind that was immersed in practical life . . . , that wished always to show you how anything was done and under what disadvantages. [I] liked the spirit of justice and scientific inquiry that reigned over the *Commentaries*, the geographer's curiosity and the Roman adaptiveness that circumvented the enemy by a study of his own techniques.' (James Agee had in *Let Us Now Praise Famous Men* less coolly circumvented enemy documentarists by more violently assaultive study of their techniques.) 'Catiline' and 'Caesar' have by now become points of reference in a consideration of the strategies as well as the values to be pursued in prose style and narrative demeanor, simultaneously with their pursuit in personal development.

'Justice, good will, moderation, and *uncommon fidelity*' − virtues demonstrated by Diviciacus in service of Caesar in Gaul − 'why should these substantives of virtue have stirred the Seminary's Catiline,' a protagonist moreover who has disclaimed these traits elsewhere in *Memories* while telling other 'stories' of her effort to aquire them? Part of the answer she has already provided in her response, complicated by the 'stirrings of maturity,' to her own speech as Catiline. As stylist and in moral sensibility, the narrator of *Memories* considers that she has matured from her younger self, able now to temper the excesses and judiciously direct the intensities of 'Catilinarian' energy. But part of the answer also lies in the fact that in part of her being McCarthy remains Catiline, embattled with but also (therefore?) attracted to an opposite image of herself. 'Hail Caesar!' she intones, in lasting literary fealty as well as in jocular dismissal of her adolescent 'crush' on the conqueror. But when she says 'Little as it meant to me then, I cannot get it out of my mind today that Catiline, in his brilliant costume, was a murderer,' she is not only passing judgment on the figure she formerly portrayed. She is also, in her mind today, back in that costume then, capable if not in fact of murder, at least in fiction (with its accumulated claims to truth in this book) of Catiline's 'demagogic vanity,' and with some awareness of its potential consequences in real life as an American, rather than imaginary existence as a Roman. The 'Figures in the Clock' of the title of this portion of *Memories* move in and out of the works 'in response to atmospheric pressures.' So too these interlocking yet opposed self-projections by McCarthy extend their shifting pressures of personality out into the volume as a whole, as a sense of 'Huck' and 'Tom' informs even those works by Clemens in which those characters do not appear.

'There is always one theme in Mary McCarthy's fictions,' writes Alfred Kazin, with something like her presumption to identification with Caesar in mind: 'none of these awful people is going to catch *me*. The heroine is always distinctly right, and gives herself all possible marks for taste, integrity and indomitability. Other people are somehow material to be written up.'[4] Whether or not this accurately characterizes a general pattern of personal investment in her fictional heroines, we have seen her *re*investment of one heroine from a novel in her self-portrayal in *Memories*, in the case of Martha Sinnott of *A Charmed Life*. A reader of McCarthy's *non*fiction subsequent to *Memories* is also often struck by the extent to which self-portrayal can be central to her treatment of a subject. The inward play of her imaginative response is as frequently the substance as it is the servant of her outwardly avowed literary purpose, or the onward momentum of her narrative line. The intellectual, aesthetic and (pre-eminently) moral assurance of her self-characterization exerts defining pressure on her materials, be they those of the polemicist or critic, the social historian or reporter on immediate public events. This pressure of personality relates more than distinguishes, indeed fuses into a form of autobiographical narrative continuous with *Memories*, these various literary roles, along with a number of their respective techniques.

Having responded through his writings to Caesar's personality, she had also then responded to the human drama on a larger, public stage embodied in the *Gallic War*. Nearing 'the great rising of Book VII,' her teacher 'began, by slow degrees, to prepare me for something painful that was coming . . .':

> To her, this rising was a tragedy, a tragedy that Caesar anticipated and tried to avert up to the very last moment. It was a

tragedy not only in the sense that a high civilization was crushed, to the accompaniment of many casualties, when a peaceful assimilation might have been managed, but because a noble nature was brought to dust in it.[5]

The noble nature was that of Vercingetorix. But just as McCarthy's fascination with Caesar in *Memories* shifts from the personal to the public, without loss on the public plane of personal involvement, so in shifting from the self-inquiries of *Memories* to the study of public issues in much of her more recent nonfiction, she brings with her the persona shaped in the earlier book. This seems particularly true of *Vietnam* (1967), *Hanoi* (1968) and *Medina* (1972), collected with an essay (like an interchapter in *Memories*) dealing further with the circumstances of their composition in *The Seventeenth Degree* (1974). In these short books about the American presence in South Vietnam, the impact of the war on North Vietnam, and the psychic as well as legal aftermath in America of the killing at My Lai, McCarthy traces the rising of a modern tragedy, some measure of the human cost of which was perhaps avertable up to the last of many moments of political decision throughout. She also writes of an American sense of national nobility, if not of the noble nature of individuals. Captain Medina to say the least is to her no Vercingetorix, but she sees the collective American moral nature as, if not brought to dust, at least irrevocably damaged, for reasons extending far back in time and far beyond the terrain of Southeast Asia.

McCarthy originally wrote much of this material, as she had the main essays in *Memories*, for magazine publication, each set of articles reworked into a volume before the next set was composed. Read as a continuous sequence (she clearly came to see them as one), the books convey a coherent narrative of experience absorbed as much as observed, and of McCarthy's shaping personality correspondingly shaped. As the material accumulates and expands, the circumference of her attention progressively contracts (as the titles suggest), from the abstract illusions underlying American involvement in Vietnam, to a more geographically and humanly specific consideration of the view from Hanoi, finally finding in Medina a 'juncture-point' of the war's contradictions, more accessible to the novelist's than to the reporter's eye. So also one's sense of McCarthy's personal investment in her accounts progressively intensifies.

'Facts,' those she accepts as given at the outset and reaffirms at the end, together with those she discovers or revises along the way, gradually become internalized, their secure possession by the reader increasingly a matter of McCarthy's *self*-possession. The 'integrity' of the novelist-heroine impugned by Kazin is in these works to be understood as a process through which the author-protagonist integrates the factuality of her material with her own subjectivity, strives to complete herself in relation to it. This process, moreover, depends for rhetorical and moral persuasiveness on McCarthy's willingness − amply demonstrated in *Memories* − to risk through self-questioning the safe certainty which Kazin suggests is an *un*questioned premise of her fictional self-projections. She *is* in these books, whatever the case in her novels, 'caught' in situations in which her *own* 'awfulness' or innocence eventually becomes a central issue, one determinant among many of the 'truthfulness' of her reportage. In order to 'write up' others she must, in the literary situation evolving around her here, write up herself.

'I confess that when I went to Vietnam . . . I was looking for material damaging to the American interest,' she states in the opening sentence of *Vietnam*. It is hardly an apology, despite the confessional note (any more than her *mea culpa* in *Memories*), though its tense allows for shadings between the anticipated and the directly observed facts. McCarthy's own 'interest' as a writer at the outset is to document further an existing case against the war, the prosecution of which case indeed concerns her throughout all three books.

From the start, however, there are signs of more subtle problems and possibilities involving self-representation. Personal pronouns gradually become charged, stress-points in a structure through which McCarthy begins to negotiate the issue of her own Americanness in relation to American acts or attitudes she is attacking. This web of self-reference is further complicated as it expands by the developing relationship between author and reader, a relationship with its own points of presumed contact or tension. 'I' and 'you,' 'we' and 'they' − the problematical quality as well as the grammatical necessity of such designations emerges early as a condition of McCarthy's probing of relations between her subjective resources and her objective aims. Early suggestions also arise of a mind deflected inward by, as well as reacting outward to, its encounters; of involuntary as well as deliberate forays into the personal past for perspective on the national present. As she grows accustomed to the 'sight and sound of . . . massed American might' in Saigon, an earlier notebook entry registering her initial shock at the open display of power loses its meaning for her, 'as when a fragment of a dream, written down on waking, becomes indecipherable.' Similarly, but in reverse, 'buried fragments of . . . personal history' start to work their way — like bits of shrapnel through flesh — toward the surface of her text, blending with the impressions which summon them, and which they help to decipher.

Though 'the mind cannot excavate what Saigon must have been like "before"' the overwhelming American presence (she does not extensively deal with the issue of earlier French involvement), McCarthy's mind does attempt, and her prose begins to express the energy of the effort, to penetrate the past so as to grasp the present. At times she wishes to explode by the force of her disgust the Americanized surface, verbal strategy appropriate to a cultural impact as violently imposed as any bomb-crater. At times it is a matter of 'excavating' an imaginative truth by careful siftings of immediate observation through memory or association, the strategy now an 'archaeological' procedure, like that in *Memories*, of patient verbal brushwork. Sometimes too, an alternative image floats mirage-like beyond the actual scene, as when she sees in Hue, an imperial capital, the 'dignified and melancholy' face of an older Vietnam. Or, having observed that 'war, a cheap form of mass tourism, opens the mind to business opportunities,' as when her own mind opens 'as if on a movie screen' to a scene of fast-buck real-estate development, Manifest Destiny and the California Dream revived and reconverging on Saigon.

Such self-investments in her subject matter are intermittent in *Vietnam*, prospects rather than resources fully exploited. They illuminate from the edges, rather than from the core, arguments which finally focus more abstractly on the paradox of American powerlessness to leave a situation predicated on American power. But even some of McCarthy's conventional argumentation, given these bursts of participatory energy, reflects the growth of a persona within the assertion of a viewpoint. The misuse of language by military and political figures, deliberately distorting or unwittingly revealing the truth, is a recurrent theme. But each instance of linguistic mutilation she cites, while it contributes to her case, seems also to irritate her own mental and moral tissues, to provoke her toward personal confrontation and thus to stimulate one's sense of her personal voice. The listless boredom of Saigon, even in the midst of frantic profiteering, serves McCarthy's polemic purpose as an index of the war's venality and the emptiness of its professed aims. Yet such evidence of incuriosity — and 'in this half of the century Americans have become very incurious,' like deadened language both cause and effect of our paralysis in Vietnam? — seems beyond its argumentative function to abrade her own curiosity, to incite questions spilling over the channels of her specific case. Abhorring the vacuums in the mental and moral life around her, and in a way easily transcending the grammarian's or the moralist's narrower complaints, McCarthy's personality begins naturally enough to fill those vacancies, there to gain new purchase, literary-technical as well as mental and moral, on questions of increasing personal urgency.

Thus, oddly yet significantly, *Vietnam* culminates in a question put by an emergent self just *before* a final chapter, 'Solutions,' argues the impossibility of solutions without some break in the pathology of official attitudes. McCarthy notes that repeating certain acts (i.e. bombing strikes) with foreknowledge of their consequences (i.e. civilian casualties) while denying those consequences (i.e. by first denying they occurred and then terming them 'accidents') suggests 'an extreme and dangerous dissociation of the personality.' Then she asks, 'Is this what is happening with the Americans in Vietnam?' The personality of Captain Medina, registering at close range in McCarthy's imagination, eventually affords a point of interpretive leverage as to just how dangerous to American moral sanity, not to mention the physical well-being of the Vietnamese, such dissociation might be. (McCarthy does not address the question of the 'civilian' status of the villagers at My Lai, not that it would fundamentally change her sense of the meaning of the Medina trial.) Here at the end of *Vietnam*, however, 'Solutions' can only restate, not explore, the problem. In *Hanoi*, by contrast, the questionings of a more prominent self are from the first more central to the shape, tone and pace of the discussion, borne inward by the pressure of personal implications: 'Quite a few of the questions one does not, as an American liberal, want to put in Hanoi are addressed to oneself.'

'He used his imagination,' McCarthy quotes an officer as saying with a smile about a description by John Steinbeck of a Vietnamese hamlet's revival through American aid, a village she sees in *Vietnam* to be still a ghost town. Her own imagination in *Hanoi*, working on her first impressions of the North, she feels to be that of an 'outsider.' This is partly a matter of being a guest from the 'other side,' and thus out of politeness as well as prudence asking fewer questions than are actually being generated in her mind. It is also, however, a self-characterizing stance, embraced for its strategic advantages much as Adams in the *Education* or Mailer in *The Armies of the Night* or *Of a Fire on the Moon* affects self-effacement in the interest of self-assertion. She is just as glad, for example, that an invitation to visit the front lines is withdrawn; not simply because of physical danger (though she admits to fear), nor even altogether because 'the meaning of a war, if it has one, ought to be discernible in the rear, where the values being defended are located'; but also because her sense of 'evidence,' her sense *of* those values in this case, is more and more a matter of interior resonances. The 'farfetchedness' of evidence becomes in a way an argument for its admissibility:

(Does the reader feel that some of these comparisons are farfetched? They mostly come from my notebook and were taken down on the spot, hurriedly, lest I forget . . . . A curious and maybe important thing about North Vietnam is just this historical resonance. What seems strange and new there at the same time has an insistent familiarity: 'Who or what does this suddenly remind me of?' Farfetched may be the right word.)[6]

The depth or distance from which a personalizing connection is made, always assuming that such evidence survives the journey, seems still to 'work,' is its validation. One thinks of Mailer's metaphorical reachings for subjective proof, and notes a reference to Mailer in *Hanoi* which, though mildly disparaging, seems also to constitute a link such as that between Adams and Aquarius,[7] a momentary recognition of shared literary situation, else why the reference at all?

The effect of this emphasis on the 'outsider's' sensations is an increase in interior pressure, a consequent quickening and deepening of mental flow. 'There is a good deal in North Vietnam that unexpectedly recalls the past,' and buried fragments of personal history which glinted briefly in the earlier book now well up, recohering as they come, into passages of commingling observation and recollection. These substances of self (like substantives of Caesarian virtue in *Memories*) seep into the forms and shadings of the immediate reality, altering while taking possession of them, yet rendering them persuasively in their factual existence as well. Crossing the Red River by makeshift means recalls blown bridges in Italy after World War II, 'Bombed by Liberators' scrawled in Italian throughout regions thus liberated. (In *Memories* Dumnorix's dying cry, that he was free and of a free state, 'have echoed reproachfully in my mind, particularly during [World War II], when they merged with the screams of other Gauls, other patriots and Resistance leaders who failed to keep faith with the conqueror.') Bomb-pitted roadways merge strangely with girlhood memories of Minnesota, giving over in turn to a sense of relationship between the 'pioneer' aspect of North Vietnamese countryside and an earlier era in American life. A pioneer ethic and mentality then become keys to McCarthy's interpretation of the strength of North Vietnamese resistance, or of the relative liveliness of Hanoi compared to Saigon's lassitude. Hanoi's trees and lakes summon references to Minneapolis and Warsaw, as if close attention to natural facts could obliterate political geography along with ideology, carving common human ground out of personal association. *Ban* trees in mountains near Hanoi, linked with memories of Dien Bien Phu, blend in imagination with the poppies of Flanders; an image then somehow arising in a reader's mind of Khe Sanh, treeless and flowerless from shelling, already more a memory than a place, the more so if in fact reclaimed by vegetation. An aura of 'before' and 'after' thus enfolds each 'now' — more than mere nostalgia on McCarthy's part, an interpretive pulse in each case felt in the text.

Sometimes the mental surface is more violently disturbed by the upsurge of thought, detonations from within as much as the threat of B-52s from above disrupting the composure of McCarthy's 'I': 'I was aware of a phychic upheaval, a sort of identity-crisis, as when a bomb lays bare the foundations of a house thought to be modern.' Presented as a gift with a ring and comb fashioned from the metal of a downed American plane — each engraved 'like a wedding ring' with the date of downing — she is inwardly appalled, sure of the givers' friendly rather than ghoulish intent, but able neither to wear, reject nor discard the items. The ring, though hidden, 'kept troubling my mind, making me toss at night, like an unsettled score.' The comb, at the time more innocuous than the ring, she realizes as she writes has never touched her hair. 'Mysterious.' It seems at first just a matter of manners, but 'what was it that, deeper than politeness, was urging me' to refuse the gift?

Maybe the premonition that if I once put it on, I could never take it off; I could not sport it for the rest of my stay and then get rid of it as soon as I left the country — that would be base. Yet equally repugnant to my nature, my identity, . . . would be to be wedded for life or at least for the duration of this detestable war to a piece of aluminum wreckage from a shot-down U.S. war plane . . . . But if respect for the feelings of others forbade my junking it in a wastebasket . . . , then there was no sea deep enough for me to drop it in. I had to keep it.[8]

The paradigmatic 'pattern' of McCarthy's first Communion in *Memories* is clearly apparent here. So too is her drive, more appropriately if no less consistently apparent in the context of *Memories* than in Kazin's view of her novels, toward self-justification. But just as there is no real solution in *Hanoi* to this immediate problem of social behavior, there is no clear solution to McCarthy's vaguer sense of a problem of symbolic meaning. Wedded here indeed (as Mailer was 'Wedded to horror' in the symbolic aftermath of Hemingway's death) to a personal predicament of association with and aversion to the war, she represents the national dilemma. She can 'settle the score,' solve the 'mystery,' only, if at all, by an inquiry into the nature of her responsibilities as a writer in relation to the material of these volumes. Her psychic upheaval has created a problem of literary identity as well. Whereas *Vietnam* concluded with 'Solutions' which were no solutions, the remainder of *Hanoi* moves toward conclusion in 'First Principles.'

In search of such principles, McCarthy at one point determines that 'the best course was to avoid reminiscences, black out large compromising areas of my personal past, and concentrate on the present.' There is momentary comfort in the resumption of a straightforward reportorial task, just as she feels 'more comfortable' in the geometry classroom of a school she visits, conic sections on the blackboard proclaiming a 'disinterested world of pure forms,' her sense of impure interests and political forms on both sides of the De-Militarized Zone momentarily soothed. Yet the comfort evaporates in the failure of her notion of geometry as a 'binding universal' to survive its translation to the students. And the history classroom reactivates an interior discomfort, an abrasion as well as stimulation of imagination, as instruction on the tactics of Dien Bien Phu contends with her notion of history as 'firmly set in the past, beyond partisan passion,' and thus 'close to art; it is a "story."' (She seems to forget her own passionate participation in the Gallic War of *Memories*, yet she also in that book obviously considers such study a binding universal.) The 'story' she is writing here, with different and still-developing closenesses to both history and art, is driven by its discomforts, a constant process of self-adjustment to a medium she is in the process of discovering. Feeling 'compromised' by certain subjective materials (though this schoolhouse sequence is in the end as rooted in the personal as any other), McCarthy now tends to concentrate on the present at the expense of reminiscence. But the present has an 'as I write' immediacy, is in fact the book's compositional present, focusing attention on the act of writing up the event as much as on the event itself. She herself is more clearly the event; far from blacking herself out, she writes increasingly from within her compromised condition, examining an image in the mirror of her own words.

To return to 'First Principles,' then, is to return to oneself as an irreducible resource, and this concluding chapter largely consists of a personal presence, an author-protagonist's focus on the inward outcome of the trip north. Just as the North Vietnamese find that certain basic elements, all else failing, will serve — water as well as plasma or saline will allay shock in bomb victims, bamboo will replace blown steel bridges — McCarthy tests basic elements of self for use in her literary predicament. North Vietnamese archaeological projects, she had noted with surprise, continued despite the war, as if Bronze Age relics, by documenting the depth of Vietnamese cultural roots, could further reinforce the collective identity and so aid the war effort. McCarthy, an archaeologist in these texts of the subjective truth embedded in sediments of fact, had felt her own 'foundations' bared by the shock of her journey, in the sense of her literary journey through all three books. Now she feels herself excavating at still deeper levels, coming on clues to change as well as continuity in personal identity:

Some vague assurance of superiority, not personal but generic, had been with me when I arrived; it was the confidence of the American who knows himself to be fair-minded, able to see both sides, disinterested, objective, etc., as compared to the single-minded people he is about to visit. To be just to myself and to those who brought me up, I think I do possess those qualities, though perhaps not as much as I imagine. They are the fossil remains of the Old America . . . . That is how the heroes and heroines of Henry James saw themselves.[9]

Like Adams pondering his kindship with *Pteraspis* or *Terebratula* in the *Education*, McCarthy looks back over sudden interior vistas at a 'fossilized' moral and literary type, traces of Caesar's 'severe magnanimity' faintly visible below the Jamesian stratum. In the process, she casts herself (as in *Memories*) as heroine in a way which to some degree neutralizes Kazin's view, seeming both to anticipate and supersede his point. She both is and is not the same. As with Strether in *The Ambassadors* or Isabel in *The Portrait of a Lady*, alteration in self-awareness is no absolute transformation, nor is McCarthy interested in such a change. A shift in internal perspective is, however, a critical factor in how one perceives and conducts one's ambassadorial or marital, or indeed one's reportorial, business.

Her 'avowed purpose' in going north 'was to judge, compare, and report back,' again like Strether's in first going to Paris, again based on the 'confidence' of an earlier American type. But the claim to objectivity, the certainty of being able to write out of that aspect of oneself, has over the course of the narrative been 'shrinking,' not so much disappearing as being compressed by experience into a different substance, a 'cherry stone' of self in which acknowledgment of complex personal interest is the prime literary source: 'a subject, an "I," asserting itself.'

It is not simply a matter of sympathy with the North, though McCarthy believes that 'the truth, renamed by us "propaganda," has shifted to the other side,' began to in fact with our first violation of linguistic truth in the term 'advisers.' (She notes as well that the regenerative themes of Western nineteenth-century fiction are central to North Vietnamese popular art, as if surfacing there after having faded here; the 'Free World,' to judge by its [twentieth-century] artifacts,' now *un*free to choose another course in the conflict.) Emersonian in her faith in language as a bonding between inner and outer realities, an integrating or dissociating force in individual or national personality depending on its use, she seeks throughout these works, as throughout *Memories*, to 'hold onto my identity' through close attention to words. It more importantly 'came down to this: if I was an unsuspicious source . . . so far as a wide American public was concerned, this meant I was a suspicious character to all who mistrusted that public's standards and morality – including myself.' In 'How It Went,' the essay accompanying these texts in *The Seventeenth Degree*, McCarthy speaks of novelists as 'curious – in both senses – beings,' whose impressions, whatever their biases, are therefore received with curiosity by readers. 'But there was something that went deeper,' she continues, 'than the mere feeding of curiosity in the reader-storyteller relation. I had the conviction (which still refuses to change) that readers put perhaps not more trust but a different kind of trust in the perceptions of writers they know as novelists from what they give to the press's "objective" reporting . . . . This believe of mine was what was prompting me . . . to go' to Vietnam. Her 'novelistic powers of observation' felt here in *Hanoi* to be suspect, by herself if only for the moment, *we* have seen her novelist's energies and instincts increasingly enlisted in self-characterizing episodes of involvement and response. 'The plea of being elsewhere, at my blameless typewriter, when the crime was committed would not stand up any more for an American writer.'

If her 'I' is presumptuous here in speaking for all American writers, the presumption seems at least partially justified by an effort of self-confrontation at least as important as the physical journey to Hanoi. A trip initially undertaken for 'my own peace of mind' – as if using one's literary influence might help end the war and restore one's life to normal – becomes an inward search for 'my own salvation,' the fossil remains of a Catholic girlhood yielding up the phrase. Salvation, such as it is for this American writer confronting the interior consequences of an American 'crime' (later type of both the child and the adult brooding on her first Communion), consists in possessing the aluminum ring, never forgetting even if not wearing it. (The aluminum POW bracelets so popular for a time tended rather to be conspicuously worn, then easily discarded.) McCarthy knows – along with the heroes and heroines of Henry James despite her invocation of them earlier as representing a different view – that 'Nothing will be the same again, if only because of the awful self-recognitions,' not least her own, that 'the war has enforced.'

A brief epilogue to *Hanoi* foreshadows *Medina* with something of the same eerie prescience suggested by the similarity (and deep difference) between McCarthy's gift ring and the bracelets subsequently figuring in the American public symbol system. Learning on her way back from Hanoi of the deaths of two German doctors of her acquaintance in Hue, their bodies identified from a mass grave, she reflects on the impossibility of knowing what happened. Rumors hopelessly conflict; she is 'somewhat suspicious of American stories of mass graves,' but recognizes that 'no army or guerilla band fails to commit an occasional act of senseless, stupid butchery.' There can be no excuse – 'it happened and cannot be retraced.' Only time may eventually avenge or absolve, conferring at least the amnesty of historical distance.

All this before the retracing of My Lai, before confusions surrounding and pervading the resultant courts-martial as symbolic explorations of the question of American guilt in the war as a whole. Later, having contracted to report on the trial of Medina, McCarthy brings to this ostensibly straightforward assignment, through the continuing assertion of her cumulatively shaped 'I,' her experience as author-protagonist of the earlier books, including *Memories*. Even without the epilogue to *Hanoi*, having travelled a psychological as well as geographical distance to and from Vietnam, she would inevitably be drawn to this dimension of American self-encounter on home ground.

The shortest of the three volumes, *Medina* requires only brief discussion, less because of length as such than because it is undivided by chapters, a single statement of the protagonist self as well as an observer's report. If the personal presence seems more static than in *Hanoi*, it is because McCarthy now seems the possessor rather than the pursuer of her literary soul *vis-à-vis* the war as a literary subject. She knows who 'I' is, having learned through the process of the preceding texts, at some psychic risk and cost. My Lai, moreover, however shocking, is of a piece with what she has long known now about the nature of this war, neither more nor less atrocious than other incidents before and since in which action has been 'dissociated' from awareness of consequences. By now long familiar too with her personal symbol of the need for an unbroken circle of relationship among will, act and result – her ring – she is interested here in individual and institutional reaction to some comparable test of acknowledgment of responsibility. If she casts a cold eye on Medina, if her voice in *Medina* is more dispassionate than in Hanoi – as it becomes apparent that the test of acknowledgment will fail on the collective as well as the individual level – she is not necessarily less personally present than she has been.

The courtroom atmosphere is well known to McCarthy's persona, an atmosphere of boredom as pervasive and enervating as August heat in Georgia, where the court-martial takes place, or in Saigon. Seeming to fix the participants in tableaux of ennui, threatening to numb an observing intelligence, this atmosphere nevertheless begins to communicate its message. She is rasped into noticing fragments of the truth which the proceedings seem designed to ignore more than to deny. (The only two witnesses who strike her as trying to come to terms with the enormity of the event seem to her, by contrast, to rasp the nerves of the court.) She feels a 'growing and eerie familiarity' with the procession of witnesses, the drone of predictably formulaic exchanges, as if having seen and heard them before, as indeed she has, in other places and voices, in the first two volumes on Vietnam. (The same 'eerie' sensation of *déjà vu* informs McCarthy's later articles on the Watergate hearings, also issued in a book as *The Mask of State*, but without the same degree of reliance on self-portrayal as controlling technique.) The 'inescapable truth of a massacre' slowly accretes, in the 'interstices' rather than the substance of testimony on both sides. In ironically direct proportion, so it seems through the narrative moldings of McCarthy's mind, the conviction inescapably forms that the Army is conspiring to undercut its own case. The 'sides' of a question which is never really posed in court ('Ask Me No Questions' . . .) crumble together, unable to enforce or bear the weight of a true answer. The trial rather than the truth is the institutional perception of duty. Moral issues 'fade' and the trial turns in narrowing spirals of technicality down to a point of exhausted impasse − the public too by now bored with the possibility of symbolic self-recognition, if beneath such boredom still fearful of it. 'Medina would be acquitted; the law would be satisfied, and God alone knew the larger truth.'

As the 'character' occupying this point of moral impasse, Medina presents McCarthy with a minimal, opaque surface on which to exercise her novelistic powers. Watchfully inert, stirring only on defense, his hooded eyelids veil his expression as his testimony veils his thoughts and feelings. Yet McCarthy seems not to regret the absence of display as a source of clues to her imagination. Further testimony of the same sort would only interfere, as 'intelligence' has interfered with intelligence in Vietnam (and Watergate). Though convinced of Medina's guilt, she is not mainly interested in defining categories or apportionments of blame. The inhabitants of My Lai, like the German doctors in Hue, are beyond the reach of such determinations.

What McCarthy sees in Medina, or appropriates to him out of her own need to understand what everyone involved seems determined not to comprehend (or comprehends and thus determines to deny), is a 'juncture-point' of confusions and forces, between the abstractions of policy and the actions of individuals. Midway in the chain of command, midway at My Lai between precise observational patterns flown by aircraft over the hamlet and the sudden chaos on the ground, midway indeed in the legal proceedings (Lieutenant Calley's case having been 'completed' with none of the basic issues resolved) − Medina is available to McCarthy as a 'transition figure' through whom the military abstraction was not so much distorted as inevitably translated into the human horror. 'A figure of speech, overworked, takes its revenge by coming to life,' she had written in *Hanoi* of the dehumanized reiterations of propaganda on both sides. A moral vocabulary without reference to consequences, its weaponry in words as well as ordnance, will eventually have the consequences it denies.

Whatever any individual's intent or lack thereof − and a lack, a vacancy of conscious will is for McCarthy at the heart of American moral failure in the war − the incident thus 'bears the mark of a particular personality,' Medina's but not his alone. And again the failure of correspondence between the will and the deed is in the word. As elsewhere in these books, words '"accidentally" . . . broken loose from their common meanings' alert McCarthy to interior conditions. The most central, if not the most subtle, of these in *Medina* is the coming of 'remorse' to mean a desire for revenge, a need to strike in panic or despairing rage against a sense of being trapped, the moral shell-shock of the entire war thus invested in the term:

> Calley in his own trial spoke of a pre-My Lai 'remorse for losing my men in the mine field, remorse that those men ever had to go to Vietnam, remorse for being in that sort of a situation where you are completely helpless.' In short, he felt regret for things that were not his fault, and the sad sensation . . . was presented as an excuse for mass murder, about which his conscience, so he said, was at ease.[10]

So too, 'as heard in the Medina trial, conscience seemed to be chiefly an organ of self-justification . . . . That attitude was the precipitating cause of the massacre,' perhaps as well of the decade-long conflict, its roots still other decades long, for which My Lai must at least partially stand.

Mary McCarthy's 'particular personality,' an opposite view of both public and private conscience the key to the shape of its literary mark in her books on the war, has been felt throughout as the precipitating agent of her narrative. Toward the end of *Memories of a Catholic Girlhood*, probing through the figure of her grandmother in Seattle 'into my earliest, dimmest memories, and into the family past behind' them, she had said that in her grandmother's character 'may lie the key' to a 'mystery back of the story I have already told' in the essays leading up to 'Ask Me No Questions.' The mystery remains unsolved in its genealogical details, as a reader by this point knows it must. Its solution as well as its narrative first principle lie instead in the condensations, within atmospheres of elusive fact, of her fictional as well as autobiographical self-creation. One's sense of her effort to sculpt as much as to 'hold onto my identity' intensifies in her realization that while her grandmother's sons are living they are without issue. 'After them, the Preston name will be extinct,' an orphan's sense of being orphaned again (the grandparents in Minneapolis had long since ceased to bear her any 'real' relation) aligning her once more with the remains of an Older America.

On the last page of *Memories*, McCarthy also realized that her grandmother has forgotten 'the word for mirror,' a mental disconnection of word from object as natural in her great age as the moral dissociation of word from act is fatally unnatural in *Medina*. With tenderness to match the severity of persona at the close of the trial, yet also with a sense of this as the imaginative moment of both reorphaning and self-completion, she comprehended the fact of her grandmother's senility. Now at the end of her personal narrative of Vietnam, a final 'Amen' bears witness to a chapter of experience uneasily sustained, also bearing a reader back to the words of old Latin hymns. The strands of her being thus seem, ring-like, to make these several volumes one.

6

The Stone House: Edmund Wilson

> Much of the time I am quite by myself in an interior which is now all my own.
>
> *Upstate*

'I sit here in this old house alone,' says Edmund Wilson by way of beginning his prologue to *Upstate: Records and Recollections of Northern New York*, a 'book about that part of the world which is partly regional history and partly a personal memoir,' as he put it in a letter to Joseph Alsop.[1] Wilson's mood in the prologue is one of weariness and withdrawal, of himself as a relic of a time when the house had more meaning as a 'family center.' He feels himself forced inward in some final way by changes which, already well advanced in America at large, are finally overtaking the Talcottville to which his family came in the late eighteenth century, and where the house itself was built in 1800–4.

The buoyancy and enthusiasm concerning the writing of *Upstate* evident in Wilson's letters during and after the year to which he assigns the prologue, 1969,[2] would suggest that this prefatory mood is highly strategic. It may be as true to say, however, that these letters contain the strategies of self-expression appropriate to the various relationships they represent, and therefore to locate in this opening section part of the personal bedrock on which the book is built. As for Adams in the *Education*, Wilson's narrative tactics in *Upstate* become in the process of composition itself increasingly determined by inward shifts in his own perspectives as author-protagonist. In a sense somewhat different from, yet fundamentally the same as, that in which Joan Didion would later say (referring to herself as persona as well as to the art of Georgia O'Keefe) '*Style is character,*'[3] Wilson progressively inhabits as much as he manipulates this work's several modes, just as he progressively feels his consciousness 'fill the house.' *Upstate* is in its entirety, random and rambling as some of its ostensibly 'diaristic' entries may be, a book as substantially and coherently revealing of its author's private self in relation to his public presence, in relation also to the America of his time, as the old stone house is eloquent as to the history of its surroundings.

The introductory premise, not unlike Adams's 'posthumous' self-positioning, is that the

> memories of the past, the still lingering presences of the family, which so haunted me when I first came back here, have mostly evaporated. Although I have made new and interesting friends, my life up here now seems thinner. Here I am in the northern countryside, still beautiful but now somewhat empty, incapacitated physically . . . .
> Is the writing of this Talcottville book a last effort to fill a vacuum?[4]

The prologue's posing of the question seems rhetorically to imply that since 'all the old ghosts are gone' the vacuum must go at least largely unfilled, that it is simply too late to do more than reflect briefly, before one's own demise, on the spirit of a vanished age. (Wilson was seventy-six when *Upstate* appeared, and died at seventy-seven in 1972.) The cumulative act the narrative contains, however, is one in which such 'evaporations' of self are recondensed, not merely in reminiscence but also in reconstitution of 'my life up here,' in a personal present as well as in the familial and cultural past. Not the 'thinness' of that life, or physical incapacity — though Wilson unsparingly explores such sensations — but the substance, the 'palpability' to use James's term from *The American Scene*'s Concord sequence, of particular kinds of imaginative experience, is in the end Wilson's central subject. And these forms of imaginative experience are increasingly associated with the process of writing this particular book. Neither the infirmities of age nor the sense of local and national disintegrations of society, nor indeed of metastases in the American body politic seeming already to have brought about an alien culture as well as promising a malignant future, are glossed over, still less transcended, in the act of self-reformulation. But *Upstate* is, finally, a concentrated statement of personal survival, and a culminating instance of − not simply a diaristic index of − the *'recueillement'* through which in the process of his other major books he forged a new relation of identity to purpose while absorbing the information on which each book was based. Wilson's *recueillement* is in this sense similar to James's inward reach for a *point de repère* in *The American Scene*, a way not only of re-entering the past but also, and primarily, of reasserting the leverage gained there on the present.

In *Upstate*'s early chapters, preceding the selections from his diary-notebooks of 1950−70 which he prepared with interpolations to form the body of the text, Wilson is often drawn away from orderly résumé of his ancestors' settlement in Talcottville and the town's history, into essays on various aspects of the region's social and religious background. Quoting extensively from original sources, he also reacts to his sources, however, and images in which he personally invests as well as more neutrally draws upon begin to cluster and gather imaginative momentum independent of their documentary function.

Wilson seems to celebrate, for example, in addition to quoting without comment from a touring missionary's diary of 1802, the observation that in the Mohawk River country it was thought 'but a small affair for a man to sell, take his family and some provisions, and go into the woods upon a new farm, erect him a house and begin anew.' Countering without subverting this emblem of independence, however, he notes the same clergyman's insight into the 'obstinate feudalism' of the landowners in settled areas, which (in words of 1802) 'must necessarily operate to debase the minds and destroy the enterprise of the settlers.' Wilson seems to share, across nearly two centuries during which the underlying socio-economic facts have not necessarily been altogether transformed, this perception as well. He goes on to identify James Fenimore Cooper (as well as Franklin Roosevelt) with the 'feudal mentality' of upstate New York, saying Cooper 'was in the habit of writing in his novels as if most of these anti-rent agitators were unscrupulous sharp-dealing New Englanders, who knew nothing of the seigneurial grand manner of New York.' Yet Wilson more favorably associates with Cooper certain current as well as childhood impressions of New York wilderness, of 'forests which beyond a point are pathless and which seem to be completely uninhabited,' or of 'hardships of this . . . isolation' and the 'backbreaking . . . defeat of the farmers by their acres.' He likens an early-nineteenth-century woodsman of whom he reads to Natty Bumppo, echoing one of Cooper's general themes in his emphasis on the problem of frontier law in connection with a quarrel between this figure and a Mohawk Indian ('There is no law here,' claims the Mohawk), and the scene from *The Pioneers* in which it is said of Natty that the 'law was never made for such as he.' The point is not that Wilson commits his memories or interprets his current impressions in terms of nostalgic images from the literary past. It is rather that Wilson is doubly involved, as participant as well as critic, recording the present as well as reading the records of the past, in the 'independent realm of dream' which he says the 'north country generates' in those who live there.

His anecdotes of 'New York Religions' or 'Hardships and Dream Pockets' — of Mormonism in Palmyra or the Oneida Community or the replicas in American woods of British country houses and Irish castles — for all the wit and sheer delight in information animating them as historical exposition, accordingly gravitate in the telling toward expression of an ambiguous sense of American cultural possibility. Some seem, like James's vision of Florida's hotel-world as an irreparably perverted Arcadia, to contain their own ironic foreclosures. Others seem more genuinely if precariously open to realization, Wilson at such moments perhaps converging with Cooper if hardly with Leather-Stocking. Fraudulent (as in Wilson's view of Mormon revelation) or otherwise (as in his sense of early upstate churches as making serious efforts toward co-existence with the Indians), images of social prospect born of personal retrospect contend and conflict, eluding Wilson's attempts (intermittent in any case) to resolve them into some sort of developmental sequence. Yet they also presage what gradually becomes a developmental principle of the narrative as a whole: calculation by the persona of his personal position in relation to directions of national drift, and corresponding assessment of the general condition in terms of his interior state. Flowing back and forth along imaginative axes linking past to present and extending conjecturally into the future, consciousness also flows directly onto the page, 'here' as well as 'now' (both terms appearing frequently throughout) 'where I am writing this.'

Often in *Upstate*, and especially in the early portions, passages occur in which Wilson seeks to reconnect this compositional

present to a sense of the past recalling for a reader James's yearning, in the New England of *The American Scene*, for the refuge
and repose of an Arcadia of the mind. This despite the fact that
Wilson is recurrently at pains to point out the differences in social
and individual temperament as well as landscape between New
England and New York, and to correct the persistent miscon-
ception that he is himself a New Englander. 'The fascination that
upper New York State could exercise upon me from my earliest
summers — so long ago now that I cannot remember when I was
first brought to Talcottville — makes it possible for me to understand its attraction' for the eighteenth- and nineteenth-century
people he has been discussing with ostensible objectivity as historian or genealogist. He recalls his boyhood sense of 'entering a
different world' when traveling first by train from Utica to Boon-
ville, then arriving in Talcottville by carriage, a version of James's
Pullman-window glass first framing and then giving way to the
view from the older conveyance:

> a country of very high skies with white clouds that reduced the
> proportions of everything else, even the rising hills; of orange
> sunsets and menacing thunderstorms; a place that was strange
> and liberating, yet a place where one was perfectly at home. I
> still felt, coming back here at thirty-five, after many years of
> almost total absence, that I was visiting a foreign country but a
> country to which I belonged.[5]

He moves in memory from this sense of first arrival, through the
impression registered after years of absence ca. 1930, to the time of
his resumption of regular visits in 1950 at the age of fifty-five after
another prolonged absence, and his inheritance of the 'Stone
House' upon his mother's death in 1951. He returns still further
toward the narrative present, 'coming back here' through imaginative time and space, collapsing as he comes these various stages of
exposure to Talcottville into the moment (ca. 1970) in which he
writes this passage — like James resurfacing modern Concord with
successive layerings of the Emersonian presence.

The result — and the climax of an early chapter — is a set of
concentric images, house within town and remembering sensibility
within house, each contained as well within circles of receding
time. At the innermost center of this design, 'the smallest social
unit, if sufficiently isolated, may assume the degrees of prestige of

a capital or a nation.' Wilson is principally referring here to the still-entrenched vestiges of the 'feudal mentality,' and his own family's participation in the pattern he had earlier criticized in the case of Cooper. But in the context, already emerging, of his identification of his life as a writer with the life of the region, the suggestion arises of a persona's imagination as the concentrated essence at the center of this paradigm. It is, in its way, an image of the Republic of Letters, a mixture of seigneurial grand manner and democratic vistas of mental reach in Wilson's sense of presiding position. In the context of this study, it is also a moment in which Wilson's comment about the interrelatedness of Talcottville society takes on a suggestion of his relations as author-protagonist to those dealt with here in surrounding chapters. In a way quite distinct from the incidental fact that Mary McCarthy was from 1938 to 1946 Mrs Edmund Wilson, having instead to do with subliminal literary-historical recognitions, 'Everybody was related to everybody else or, at no matter what distance from one another, were neighbors or very old friends.'

As the literal family chronicle amasses, however, scenes of idyllic natural beauty and images of social continuity begin to yield to scenes the specific human complexities of which Wilson approaches more closely, or feels persisting in his mind from the past. A painful encounter between an uncle and a woman he hoped to marry, for example, 'took place in the big room which is now my study. It is as if its vibrations still reach me in this room, in which I am writing.' Anxious to fill out, as if in a formally posed portrait, the 'family group' (one recalls James's Transcendentalist 'portrait-group' in Concord), Wilson nonetheless finds that leisurely characterization of people supposedly fixed in time past tends to accelerate into more fluidly dramatic narrative through which these figures live for him in time present. A chapter about Dorothy Reed Mendenhall shifts rapidly from character-sketch and description (accompanied by a photograph of a portrait) into anecdotal account of her medical training at Johns Hopkins, where she knew Gertrude Stein. This further entwines with her own autobiographical writing, and with Wilson's sense of her through those writings as well as from memories of her as 'one of my most interesting relatives.' The stone house had for her a particular if unrealized significance: she had grown up 'without a real home,' although her family lived for a time in that house under lease. When they had an opportunity to buy it, they were unable to do so, and it later passed to Wilson's mother and on to him. In imagination, and in her memoirs, it *was* her 'real home,' and as portraiture passes into the absorption of her personal narrative by his, acquiring momentum independent of his initial sketch of her, it is on such mutual home ground that Wilson presents her.

To end the chapter he eventually has to brake abruptly the momentum by which it has already spread beyond its original bounds: 'But I am going too far into the future when, in my chronological story, I have only reached the point where, emerging from a dimmer past, I can at last see our family group . . . .' The portait-group is for the moment recomposed into abstract tableau, 'the Calvinism of Great-Great Grandfather Kimball that aimed at a godly community; the Toryism of the Talcotts that tried to preserve feudal dignity; and the Jacksonian democracy of Thomas Baker, who cared little about either of these ideals, but was out to make what money and what kind of career he could. I once wanted to write a play about it.' Such a play would have contained all the counterpoised oppositions in political philosophy of a Cooper novel, or of a play by George Bernard Shaw, whom Wilson admired. Indeed, this intersection of genealogical forces might be said to condense a good deal of American social history. So also Mary McCarthy, before she knew Wilson, had once attempted a play based on family history, or the conflicts which filled the vacuum of an orphan's lack of it, on one level a drama of American cultural inheritance as well. Her dramatic impulse would both echo and be fulfilled in *Memories of a Catholic Girlhood*, her personal adaptations of Roman virtue themselves oddly echoing in Wilson's report that the motto on the Talcott crest was '*Virtus sola nobilitas.*'

One of the structures within that of diary-notebook chronology, in terms of which Wilson recommences the main body of *Upstate*, consists in his sense of *Upstate*'s narrative line as transecting and providing reflective vantage on the periods of his work on other books. He speaks of concentrating on 'what I felt the admirable solidity and balance of my coming book — *The Shores of Light* — in order to justify myself' concerning instability in his relation to his wife Elena, for whom Talcottville was isolated and 'uncongenial.' He redirects a discussion of the persistence of the town's social traditions into a consideration of proximities between past and present ('easily merged in my mind') as shown in Harold Frederic's upstate stories set during the Civil War, part of Wilson's approach to *Patriotic Gore*. He remembers reading Michelet in a certain chair at the end of a particular summer, working toward *To the Finland Station*, seeming almost still to see Michelet, with him in the room where 'I am writing this' and filling the house with 'my own work and my own mind.' He has only 'partly dispelled the past,' literary and intellectual as well as familial and territorial. As he 'now' (c. 1953) reads material leading to *The Dead Sea Scrolls*, he reaches back as well through Barrett Wendell's book on Cotton Mather 'to make connections with that end of the family,' Mather a collateral relative whose praise for Anne Bradstreet in *Magnalia Christi Americana* gives Wilson a sense of literary relationship with her too.

He seems in fact possessed, in historiographical method and philosophy, by the spirit he attributes at the start of *To the Finland Station* to Michelet (although he never sees the 'ghosts' by whom Elena is periodically disturbed in the stone house). Michelet as a writer is for Wilson, as he put it in *To the Finland Station*,

> a strange phenomenon. He is in many ways more comparable to a novelist like Balzac than to the ordinary historian. He had the novelist's social interest and grasp of character, the poet's imagination and passion. All this, by some unique combination of chances, instead of exercising itself freely on contemporary life, had been turned backward upon history and was united with a scientific appetite for facts which drove him into arduous researches.[6]

Wilson also says, in the ardor of the act of research which informs much of his work and enforces as emotionally as intellectually some of his judgments, that Michelet constitutes the most 'amazing example in literature of the expansion of a limited individual experience into a great work of the imagination.' In turning himself 'inside out in his books,' Michelet in Wilson's view produced not a narrowly personal interpretation of events, but the 'emotional design' of the modern world's emergence from feudalism. This design is 'easily referable,' without being limited, to Michelet's own experience, which in turn consists largely in an effort to relive history. It is also, according to Wilson, in the most highly serious sense a 'literary' design, and very similar to that for which Wilson strives — for all his frequent retreats into the casual diarist's role — in *Upstate*.

The 'climax of the story' in Michelet's history of France (one recalls McCarthy's mixings of 'history' and 'story,' along with those of others considered in earlier chapters here) is for Wilson in the founding of the Federations after the fall of the Bastille. So too the fulfillment of emotional design in *To the Finland Station*, its 'study in the writing and acting of history' finally an imaginative 'story' as well, is in Lenin's arrival in Petrograd. In each case an attempt to 'relive the recorded events of the past as a coherent artistic creation' first seeks, and then breaks out of, 'the pattern of art' in unfinishable quest of 'the history of the future,' in Wilson's words at the end of *To the Finland Station*. Notwithstanding that his genius had been turned back on history rather than exercising itself on contemporary life, Wilson observes on Michelet's behalf that 'One cannot care . . . about what has happened in the past and not care what is happening in one's own time.' Wilson like Jules Michelet, or rather *as* his own Jules Michelet, in *Upstate* as in his previous works brings research and an appetite for facts concerning the past to bear on contemporary American life.

In *Axel's Castle* the drama of individual as well as cultural alternatives — Axel or Rimbaud — contains 'unsuspected possibilities of human thought and art,' the book as a whole and not simply its final words constituting a question about literature yet to be written. In *To the Finland Station* Lenin 'stood on the eve of the moment when for the first time in the human exploit the key of a philosophy of history was to fit an historical lock.' The book as a whole, not simply its climactic scene, has become in the writing an act of artistic creation, even if (as Wilson acknowledges) 'later events are not always amenable to this pattern. The point is that Western man at this moment can be seen to have made some definite progress in mastering the greeds and the fears, the bewilderments, in which he has lived.' Whatever Wilson's subsequent views, this 'point' and this conception of historical 'moment' — in the sense of significance as well as that of time — remain central to the book's integrity as history *and* as art. By the time Wilson completed *To the Finland Station* in 1940, he was more skeptical as to the outcome of Russian revolutionary experiment than when he began. This resulted in an ironic shading *also* integral to the 'story,' and not in the least subversive of '1917' as symbolically crucial to the drama of the human exploit, no longer amenable to the pattern of a well-made play. (In referring in *Upstate* to the period of his 'radical enthusiasms,' Wilson is in no way disavowing the attitudes, even his presence as an author-protagonist trying to relive history, in *To the Finland Station*.) So Adams had found in '1900' a symbolic turn in the 'fable' of the mind's struggle 'like a frightened bird to escape the chaos which caged it,' the accuracy of his scientific explanations irrelevant in the end to their poetic truth, irony enhancing more than diminishing the *Education*'s imaginative power. So Mailer as Aquarius comes full circle to the rediscovery in *Of a Fire* that if human history, like the physical universe, 'was a lock, its key was metaphor rather than measure.'

The Shores of Light and Wilson's other American literary 'Chronicles,' *The Dead Sea Scrolls*, *Apologies to the Iroquois*, *Patriotic Gore* — each in a way re-enacts the pattern of research into the past for the purpose of writing and acting in the present, and thus starting to write the history of the future. Even when locked in dubious battle with governmental or literary-cultural institutions, in *The Cold War and the Income Tax* or *The Fruits of the MLA*, Wilson is driven by essentially the same desire. In *A Prelude: Landscapes, Characters and Conversations from the Earlier Years of My Life*, the life-long process of notebook-keeping shifts to a formal effort to pull this pattern inward, publication perhaps an Auction of the Mind but also a private act of self-creation. (Dickinson, for that matter, writes as one more assured of eventual, if posthumous, literary life in the world than of Heavenly Grace; Emerson's 'noble doubt' for her, at base, more like Whitman's 'terrible doubt of appearances.') And in *Upstate* what Wilson in *A Prelude* called 'episodes that consisted of interwoven elements of experience' both expand and interweave in more comprehensive mapping of inward territory.

Talcottville and Wellfleet, New York and New England, become (like Adams's Quincy and Boston) regions of the mind expressible in chartings of memory and current observation, the 'independent realm of dream' and current, complicit American actuality, the act of reading and 'the writing and acting of [personal] history.' The 'landscape outside the windows is like paintings on the walls' of the stone house,[7] the world thus pulled in as Wilson feels himself fill out the house's interior. Windows themselves become pages on which his poet friends write verses appropriate to particular rooms and directions of exposure, diamond-point script to be read from within. Wilson's mind houses similarly a map of his reading: 'I can see at any moment,' he says in *Upstate*, 'all the books in the bookcases in both of my houses.'⁸ Like Nabokov's chessboard in *Pale Fire*, the 'phantom extensions' of which both limit (because unreal) and direct (because present to the mind) the course of play, the house in Talcottville encloses and also releases Wilson's thought, its stone walls lined with the solid yet intangible tissue of his actual and inwardly re-envisioned library.

Wilson reads the American cultural situation *c*. 1970, through the writing-acting of *Upstate*'s chapters of experience (he says toward the end 'I am now living a new chapter'), as tending more and more toward the 'expiration' of values, individual and collective, he has in all his work sought to affirm. It is partly a matter of an old man's 'waning powers,' and his personal irritation at the depredation of his property, whether by easement for a highway or by 'hoodlums' who break the windows on which Louise Bogan and Stephen Spender had engraved poems. And on one level he admits that his interpretation springs from a patrician's sense of steady dispossession, such as that he had satirized in his comments on Fenimore Cooper: 'My reaction to all the things that I disapprove and dislike is that of a member of a once privileged class which is being eliminated all over the world and has very little means any longer of asserting its superior "values."' James acknowledged the same response to the future's onslaughts as witnessed from Beacon Hill in *The American Scene*. But instead of being James's 'ancient contemplative person,' Wilson in this mood claims only to be trying to become, despite increasing interference from the world at large, 'a sedate old gentleman.'

It is also a matter, however, of outrage as deep and furious as that of Clemens, running beneath the surface of a prose as meticulous and measured as that of Adams, well-bred in addition to being well-crafted, its violences of feeling ironically veiled but not wholly concealed. The tyranny of bureaucracy, the blurring and dulling effects of mass conformity, the inroads of commercial construction and the disappearance of landscape in industrial blight ('you lose the glamorous country as you come down on Utica' from Talcottville), the loss of community recurrently represented by the hoodlums — all form a general vision of decline. America is 'UNSAFE,' like 'desolate' Hyde-Clarke Hall, abandoned and fallen into disrepair in Wilson's epilogue, whereas he tries throughout the book to bring his house 'up again to this countryside,' restoring its masonry while remaking himself in narrative over the years. Having first glimpsed that glorious countryside as a boy from the train, he now feels more like Robert Lowell, for whom in 'In Memory of Arthur Winslow'

> Now from the train, at dawn
> Leaving Columbus in Ohio, shell
> On shell of our stark culture strikes the sun
> To fill my head with all our fathers won
> When Cotton Mather wrestled with the fiends from hell.[9]

To Wilson as to Lowell the shells are empty now, his mind filled too with a sense of diminished inheritance. Even the fiends envisioned by the Puritans have paled by collateral descent (like Wilson's from Mather) into the faceless agents of an 'almost all-controlling government identified with the industrial and commercial interests.' In Wilson's America as in Lowell's Union Dead, 'a savage servility/slides by on grease.' The Stone House, mortgaged in the course of Wilson's battle with the Internal Revenue Service, has in a way become Lord Weary's Castle, built (according to Lowell's note in that volume) by 'a mason good / As ever built wi' stane . . . .' Wilson himself is like a hill visible from his house, part of what was once called the Lesser Wilderness, the hill to him 'a great shaggy beast lying down with its head between its paws.'

He can still be aroused, however, and the war in Vietnam — for him both symptom and cause of the social sickness, and a major source of objection to the income tax — especially draws his wrath. He mentions the war only occasionally, toward the end of *Upstate*, yet it spreads through these chapters dealing with the later 1960s as it spread then beyond American control, pervading his consciousness even if only obliquely acknowledged. He shares, indeed he may have helped inspire, McCarthy's sense of the war as a locus, at home as in Vietnam, of linguistic and intellectual imprecision linked to moral confusion. By the same token, it remains for writers other than Wilson, perhaps of a generation more directly exposed to the actual fighting, perhaps including Michael Herr whose personal narrative of the war is the subject of the next chapter of this study, to confront Vietnam as an all-consuming American literary issue.

Wilson in the end, and at the end of *Upstate*, 'cannot foresee the future, but can only go on with my old occupations,' his epilogue looping back into prologue, into the 'here' and 'now' of his autobiographical endeavor. At times it 'seems to me strange that I am still alive and writing this diary,' his own earlier books seeming to have been written 'by someone else.' Adams and James, Howells and Clemens too, had also experienced a loss of autobiographical contact with former selves, and found, or failed to find, a means of re-establishing the narrative continuity of their lives. More often, however, Wilson continues to enact the inquiring sensibility, actively curious and open to new evidence, through which he has come to know himself, as well as the subjects of his arduous researches, over a long career. His earlier books are in this sense still seen by him as stages in a coherent journey through varying terrain under shifting conditions, even though he sometimes speaks of the Talcottville journals as displacing other projects, *Upstate* thus edging toward the center of his corpus. As *Axel's Castle* and *To the Finland Station* ended in questions about the history of the future, Wilson asks as *Upstate* concludes, 'Can I even be sure that, in the language I use, I am formulating these issues correctly? Will these terms not seem very crude to a remotely distant future? — that future I cannot wait for,' terms of self-formulation in personal narrative now among the issues.

'I am still as comfortable here,' he says, in his writing as much as in his stone-built houe, 'as I can hope to be anywhere.' This sense of location, expressed in *Upstate*'s final page, has something of the heroic finality of 'Here!' — the last word of Leatherstocking in Cooper's *The Prairie*, the last word indeed (and word *as* act) of Natty Bumppo's life. Wilson says this in a voice more like that of Adams, professing only such curiosity as might keep him 'mildly amused while my faculties are gradually decaying.' Like Adams, he also professes exhaustion by the evolutionary process of 'no one knows how many million years,' after which 'only now are we beginning a little to understand' our human consciousness. But Wilson the modernist, Wilson the contributor to and critical analyst of the chastening of American prose style,[10] knows himself in *Upstate* to be an actor in the writing of America's unexhausted romance of relation to its past. In a lettter to Louise Bogan he remarks of his family's arrival in eighteenth-century Talcottville from New England, 'I suppose it was a first Westward migration.'[11] In *Upstate*, near the house, 'the moon moving through the trees brings out a romantic wilderness that I have never felt in America anywhere else but here, and that I am always somewhat astonished still to find that I do feel.'

Frederick Exley, who might on the basis of *A Fan's Notes* (1968) and *Pages from a Cold Island* (1975) have been included in a study of twentieth-century American personal narrative, begins the latter volume with this sentence: 'At 6:30 on the morning of Monday, June 12, 1972, Edmund Wilson died of a coronary occlusion at his mother's ancestral home — "The Old Stone House" — at Talcottville, Lewis County, upstate New York, an hour's drive south from where I am putting down these words . . . .' *Upstate*, as compendium of Wilson's life in letters, is Exley's polestar throughout *Pages from a Cold Island.* Despite his disdain for Norman Mailer, as one whose 'authorized version' of himself as protagonist has lost touch with a truly literary vocation, Exley sums up Wilson's accomplishment in words Mailer might have written. To follow Wilson's example is for Exley to 'hold up to America a mirrored triptych from which, no matter in which direction America might turn, she would — to her dismay, horror, and hopefully even enlightenment — be helpless to free herself from the uncompromising plague of her own image.'[12] (Wilson would have written a purer sentence than this of Exley's, and in *Upstate* he mentions Mailer, as McCarthy did in *Hanoi*, critically yet with some recognition of Mailer's persona as having become one reflector of America's self-imagining.)

Exley's obituary observations on *Upstate* tend toward self-obituary as well. '"Home," I say,' he says near the end, '"is inside *here*." With great, grave and theatrical deliberation, I lift [the] .22 Magnum and with its blue barrel go TAP, TAP, TAP against my right temple.' *Last Notes from Home*, a projected third and final book in an autobiographical triptych, has yet to appear. With equal (if perhaps at that moment less deliberate) theatricality, Mailer in *Of a Fire* had taken Hemingway's suicide as prefiguring a decade. Wilson, less theatrically, is 'very much upset' in *Upstate* by Hemingway's death, Hemingway being for all his faults in Wilson's view — chief among them self-delusion by his own public persona — 'one of the foundation stones of my generation.' But Exley, on the last of his *Pages*, is a survivor, postponing thoughts of 'stone houses, of Elysian havens, of last islands, of places that never were' until tomorrow, and (on Christmas Day) wishing all concerned (even that 'canny old *poseur* Mr. Mailer') an ironically interrogative yet also self-affirming 'productive and splendid New Year?' John Berryman expresses, in despair in 'He Resigns,' a sense of personal terminus. 'I don't feel this will change,' he writes, referring to a feeling of emptiness and isolation;

'I don't think I will sing / any more just now . . . .'[13] Filled with a comparable sense of 'the transience of all forms of life in America' as much as with awareness that his youthful images of upstate New York 'now hardly exist,' Wilson, by contrast, nonetheless says, 'I do not think, as I did last year, that I shall sell my old place here.' He is now more like the Lowell of *Day by Day* than like the author of *Lord Weary's Castle* (Wilson once as a boy said to himself, 'No: I am not quite a poet, but I am something of the kind,' we learn from *Upstate*'s prologue). With more positive force of self-determination than his syntax at first suggests, he asserts at the last that 'I shall have to go on living, and I am glad to have had some share in . . . the life of this planet and of northern New York.' It is thus with some fullness of desire to re-enact this life that these last words of epilogue reinform the opening of Wilson's prologue: 'I sit here in this old house,' his last island, 'alone.'

Obituary assessment of Wilson's career tended in general, not only in Exley's book, to gravitate toward *Upstate* as a work not to be preferred to, but rather in which to find subsumed, the other works on which his reputation rests. Alden Whitman called it in *The New York Times* the 'personal and elegaic diary of a man growing old in the place where as a child, he had first learned he was capable of "imaginative activity and some sort of literary vocation."'[14] John Leonard, on the same page of the *Times*, referred to the Wilson of Upstate as 'the American Montaigne.' He did so with reference to a long review of *Upstate* which appeared in *The Times Literary Supplement* less than a month before Wilson died,[15] but which even when read before June 12, 1972, seemed to deal with a writer become 'a memory' yet whose mind continued to shape the nation's perception of itself. Wilson had in the writing of *Upstate*, according to the unsigned essay in *TLS*, completed his self-revision into 'literatus,' less hopeful than the Whitman of *Democratic Vistas* (or indeed the Emerson of 'Montaigne'), but no less concerned to represent — still hoping against hope also to correct — his culture. Whitman (and indeed Emerson) had for that matter sensed some of the cultural tendencies Wilson would deplore. This role, self-perpetuating in narrative out of 'constant tension between the achieved serenity of his literary judgment and the threatening complexity of his self-consciousness as an American,' is now the role through which Wilson moves with 'significance in the realm of action.'

Wilson himself doubts often enough in *Upstate* the lasting

significance of such action. The book seems to *TLS*'s reviewer to 'shiver with the portent of an advancing ice-cap,' the chill before the stupor of a cultural letting go as well as the cold of personal age. But if Wilson, like others in the chapters of this study not to mention the whole record of American writing, is 'faced with the ruins of the American Dream,' he also appears at the end of the review 'to be forgetting what we are bound to remember: that the fragments can be built with and that this fact is in some measure due to him.' Such fragments are in fact what American writers from the outset have largely used to rebuild, in successive re-envisionings of personal and collective possibility, our literature's memory as well as prophecy of our life as a people. Wilson reports in *Upstate* that he often would dream, before resuming regular occupancy of the stone house, that it lay in ruins when he came for a visit. Living in the house, and continuing to rebuild portions of its structure, he now has, 'at this moment of waking up . . . , the feeling — I think unique in my life — of a dream having literally come true, and so being now satisfactory as a real dream could not be.'

Daniel Aaron, in his introduction to Wilson's *Letters on Literature and Politics, 1912–1972*, moves beyond such mixtures of obituary and critical comment as still characterize much of the discussion of Wilson's work since his death. He does so by placing him, specifically and objectively without loss of a sense of personal friendship and collateral experience of more than one American literary and political era, in the context of his times. In 'The Author at Sixty,' from *A Piece of My Mind*, Wilson had stated, 'I have lately been coming to feel that, as an American, I am more or less in the eighteenth century — or, at any rate, not much later than the early nineteenth.' In *Upstate* he mentions reading, before bed or at breakfast, the 'memoirs of the literary life of the late eighteen-hundreds and the early nineteen-hundreds, the period in which I suppose I am most at home.' Later in *Upstate* he notes that as a 'character in one of Chekhov's plays, speaking in the late nineties, says that he is "a man of the eighties," so I find that I am a man of the twenties.' And despite the fact that *Upstate* expresses his displacement in time toward Clemen's 'drift between the eternities' of death and of never having been born, it also shows him in some ways becoming a man of the other decades in which he lived and wrote, a man not only of the twenties but of the twentieth century. This steady movement forward in time, from the *point de repère* of an eighteenth-century (or at any rate not later than early-nineteenth-century) stone house, requires as Aaron observes 'a certain kind of self-effacement, a subordination if not suppression of the personal note to facts and evidence.' The drift of Wilson's life, Aaron also rightly says, was unlike Clemens's 'away from subjectivism and romanticism and toward the external world. Hence he rejected the suggestion made to him in the twenties by Christian Gauss that he write "a *confession d'un enfant du siècle*" as "repugnant to me" and strove "to become more objective instead of more and more personal." '[16] Accordingly, writing to Joan Didion in 1971, he says he never read *Mont-Saint-Michel and Chartres* and found the *Education*, which he notes Adams himself termed his own 'dreary history,' unreadable. 'Nonetheless,' Wilson continues, 'I have found him interesting on the American politics of his period.'[17]

Yet in order to be moving always toward the external world, and back into one's own time, one must move from what Agee called 'withdrawal to source' in *Let Us Now Praise Famous Men*, what Didion calls (perhaps with Wilson in mind) 'a discipline, a habit of mind,' in work to be discussed in a later chapter. This requires a certain kind of self-assertion, on which self-effacement in the service of facts and evidence is based. Style is character, as Didion along with many others including Wilson has said. And in the 'incorruptible line' of his prose, as evident in *Upstate* as anywhere else, Wilson distills his own essential character, in the sense of his presence as protagonist as well as in that of his subordination of the personal note. He keeps (as Aaron shows, quoting the narrator in *Memoirs of Hecate County*) to 'my old solitary self, the self for which I really lived and which kept up its austere virtue, the self which survived,' surviving still in *Upstate*. Despite the achieved serenity of his literary judgment on Adams in his letter to Didion, Wilson is in this sense related − lineally it would now seem − to the author of the *Education* in consistency as well as complexity of self-consciousness as an American.

The final poem, save a set of translations, in Robert Lowell's *Day by Day* is 'Epilogue.' The poet speaks of advancing age and waning literary power, and of his need to make of life 'something imagined, not recalled.' He pursues his idea of the difference between memory and imaginative creation in terms of the difference between photography and painting:

> *The painter's vision is not a lens,*
> *it trembles to caress the light.*

> But sometimes everything I write
> with the threadbare art of my eye
> seems a snapshot, . . .
> heightened from life,
> yet paralyzed by fact.
> All's misalliance.[18]

Agee's imaginative vision had trembled in words to caress the cruel radiance of light captured by Evans's lens. Lowell, unlike Agee for whom '"rembrandt," deeplighted in gold' is resolved in the course of *Let Us Now Praise Famous Men* into 'clean, staring, colorless light,' would 'Pray for the grace of accuracy / Vermeer gave to the sun's illumination.' Wilson, his imagination activated rather than paralyzed by fact, writes in a far from threadbare prose grounded in both eye and 'I' of scenes one might say he regards photographically — 'snapshots,' if you will. Some are casually compressed to the point of being visual marginalia: 'Pleasant effect of vegetation creeping up to the house yet keeping to its limits: goldenrod, bluebells and purple asters all growing close against the stone,' flowers like Thoreau's beans defining a relation between civilized and wild more through natural process than through systematic cultivation. Some are more developed: 'I could see from my bedroom window a tree silhouetted on the mist that gave the effect of a photographic negative but with the darks and the lights interchanged. Then the light came and, pouring from behind on that night-wet world, it seemed to be drenching everything: big green elms, a field of yellow clover, and beyond it a field of brown ploughed earth, the growth of foliage along the little river, the low blue hills in the distance. Bracing, even exalting — rich and fresh and brilliant landscape now blazing with light.' Some are focused on the house as a transforming lens on the world: 'Elena said that the old glass in the panes — with its fine rippling texture — gave a silky effect to the landscape.' All, including passages of personal reflection as well as visual observation, create alliances rather than revealing misalliances between the inner and the outer life.

Lowell's poem concludes:

> We are poor passing facts,
> warned by that to give
> each figure in the photograph
> his living name.

Wilson, in the chapter of *Upstate* drawn from journals of 1959, simultaneously paints in words and records with photographic accuracy an image of himself. (One of several things 'Edmund Wilson regrets that it is impossible for him' to do, listed on a card he sent in response to requests, is 'supply photographs of himself.') Wilson's self-portrait calls to mind, if obliquely, the frontispiece photograph in the first edition of *The Autobiography of Alice B. Toklas* — Stein in the foreground, somewhat shadowed, at her writing table; Toklas in the background, clearly illuminated, in a doorway. It also suggests the conflation, as much as the confusion, of realms in *Pale Fire* — 'the false azure in the windowpane' through which the shadow of the 'waxwing slain' has in a way actually passed.[19]

> *June 4.* I sit at my little card table on which I write, in my mother's old heavily upholstered chair, and look up, after work — 6:30 — at the old framed map on the opposite wall. The glass reflects and just contains the window behind me now — the white curtains, the June green of the lilac bushes, with myself, head and shoulders, at the bottom, dim but rather darkly ruddy, the line of the mat going through my chest.[20]

The house and the writer working within, together with the surrounding verdancy of the upstate season, are allied in this image, which then resolves itself into continuing self-narration, just as in *The Autobiography of Alice B. Toklas* a reader returns to the frontispiece through a photograph at the end of the first manuscript page. The living name of the figure in *Upstate*, reflected in the glass of a map of his mind, is Edmund Wilson.

7

Debriefed by Dreams:
Michael Herr

> hardly stories at all but sounds and gestures packed with so much
> urgency that they became more dramatic than a novel . . .
>
> *Dispatches*

'He had always understood what was going to happen there, and in
that small and quiet novel, told us nearly everything.' Thus Gloria
Emerson, in her account of a recent interview with Graham
Greene,[1] reiterates a view of *The Quiet American* which has
generally prevailed since the novel's American publication in
1956. With the passage of time, and the fading in the United
States of initial criticism of *The Quiet American* as anti-
American[2] – and with the passage of the American war in
Vietnam through phases prophetically implied in Greene's portrayal of Alden Pyle – the novel has become an established point
of reference for those interested in problems of literary response to
the war. As a set of defining images, if not of elaborated arguments, it has entered the 'record' of an unquiet American era, not
necessarily terminated by American withdrawal in 1975. Along
with Greene's dispatches from the period 1952–5, or rather as the
moral and aesthetic distillation of these reports from Indochina,
The Quiet American is as likely to be cited as 'evidence' by
historians and reporters as to be lauded as exemplary by literary
critics.

Frances FitzGerald's *Fire in the Lake: The Vietnamese and the
Americans in Vietnam* mentions Greene in terms calling for the
reader's recognition of his authorship of *The Quiet American*,
which appears in her formal bibliography. Mary McCarthy, in the

course of her Vietnam reportage discussed in the previous chapter, assumes an awareness of Greene's novel as a kind of authenticating credential, Greene's difficulty in obtaining documents for travel in the United States constituting a passport to the principality of her approval. A reviewer of Robert Stone's *Dog Soldiers*, a novel only partially set in Vietnam but profoundly 'about' the war, speaks of the protagonist as driven by 'the fear that traditionally afflicts Quiet Americans in South-East Asia.' (William Lederer's and Eugene Burdick's *The Ugly American* had earlier prompted a reviewer to note that the 'authors have apparently heard of a rather more sophisticated work by Mr. Graham Greene.') In these and other instances, it is Greene the former Indochina hand and author of this particular novel, as much as Greene seen more generally in the context of a long career, who hovers ghostlike, witness to a prophecy fulfilled.[3]

Its brevity and lightness of touch, and the fact that it is as often invoked with nostalgia as with detailed analysis, have not kept Greene's novel from acquiring this authority. And it is not only what Ms Emerson calls the 'first great warning' against American involvement contained in *The Quiet American* on which its authority rests. In its capacity to seem now to have quietly told us nearly everything in 1956, the book appeals (despite, or perhaps paradoxically due to, British authorship) to a collective American yearning for a prior point of moral clarity, which developments since 1956 seemed until recently to have kept out of American literary reach.

Over the past ten years or so, however, American writers in increasing numbers have attempted to distill images of the war's private as well as public meanings, images which might fix those meanings in the national consciousness with the force of art as well as entering them in the documentary record. As we have already seen in the case of McCarthy, extending an autobiographical narrative into certain kinds of close encounter with the war, the efforts of these writers more generally have come to constitute a process of ongoing inquiry as to the appropriate terms of literary treatment. Whether the experience of Vietnam, viewed as personal encounter or as cultural collision, was so extreme as to enforce revised angles of literary approach; or whether the literary experimentations already under way in the 1960s were bound in any case to be applied to the experience of Vietnam; the problem of means in relation to ends, of literary method in relation to a subject resisting definition by literary precedent, emerges as an aspect of the subject itself.

American novels of the war by now include, among others, such works as David Halberstam's *One Very Hot Day* (1968), William Eastlake's *The Bamboo Bed* (1969), James Park Sloan's *War Games* (1971), Joe W. Haldeman's *War Year* (1972), Josiah Bunting's *The Lionheads* (1972), William Turner Hugget's *Body Count* (1973), Robert Roth's *Sand in the Wind* (1973), Robert Stone's *Dog Soldiers* (1974), Larry Heinemann's *Close Quarters* (1977), Winston Groom's *Better Times Than These* (1978), Tim O'Brien's *Going after Cacciato* (1978), and Gustav Hasford's *The Short-Timers* (1979). Despite the recurrent claim that 'there has been no real challenger to Graham Greene's aging novel' in American fiction dealing with Vietnam (an American critic here conveying a sense of simultaneous reliance on and rejection of Greene's model),[4] books such as these find their own ways of differentiating themselves from Greene's example, and from one another. As a group, they present themselves more or less traditionally as novels, without overt insistence on the issue of alternative or improvisatory genre. With differing degrees of apparent awareness of Greene, they collectively suggest a different standard of comparison – with American authors ranging from Stephen Crane to Hemingway, Mailer, Heller, and others – to the extent that they assume a continuity of literary enterprise between the war in Vietnam and earlier American conflicts. To a corresponding extent, they struggle to define and give distinctive expression to those aspects of the Vietnam experience which are distinct from other American wars.

The novels accumulate, while still relatively little read (despite National Book Awards to *Dog Soldiers* and *Going after Cacciato*),[5] and the novelists continue to reconnoiter in relatively new literary terrain. But the 'challenge' to Greene – based ambiguously on both acknowledgment and disavowal of *The Quiet American* as in some sense 'definitive' of American experience in Vietnam – has meanwhile become more apparent in American personal narratives of involvement in or exposure to the war. So also has the quest for alternative form become more pronounced, as it is in the material gathered in McCarthy's *The Seventeenth Degree*, in such works as Jonathan Schell's *The Village of Ben Suc* (1967), John Sack's *M* (1967), Susan Sontag's *Trip to Hanoi* (1968), Ronald Glasser's *365 Days* (1972), Gloria Emerson's *Winners and Losers*

(1976), Ron Kovic's *Born on the Fourth of July* (1976), C. D. B. Bryan's *Friendly Fire* (1976), Philip Caputo's *A Rumor of War* (1977), and Michael Herr's *Dispatches* (1977) — Herr's book to stand in this chapter as the example under analysis. The novel as Greene employed it was the naturally appropriate means to his ends. Just as naturally however variously, these American books fan out radially in search of new forms of literary leverage on resistant material, from a center Greene seems at once still to occupy and no longer usefully to provide.

While varying in interests and attitudes as well as in literary quality, these narratives are bound together to a degree by their mixtures of documentary with imaginative purpose, their fusions of private with public concern, their efforts to recombine the resources of several genres rather than settle into established prose patterns. Some, indeed, are excessively anxious over the threat to their originality or fidelity to the subject posed by conventional modes, ironically to the detriment of their own experimentation. Sooner or later, in pursuit of particular topics, they reflect internally on problems of literary procedure presented by new social and psychic 'information' generated by the war, and by reimportation of the war's moral environment to the United States. Questions of relationship and priority among autobiographical, reportorial, historiographical and novelistic purposes and techniques invariably, however differently, arise as aspects of the specific issues addressed. Sometimes, having surfaced, such questions are resolved into distinctive literary form. Sometimes they resubmerge, the lack of formal resolution itself often an appropriate formal reflection of the ways in which the war can resist literary treatment altogether.

These books also tend to consist of an inward questing for personal clarification of all that is confusing and chaotic in their subject. This is sought in narrative reconstitutions of a journey 'through' or 'beyond' the war, rather than in retrospection on a 'prior' clarity of insight such as that afforded by Greene's novel. Perhaps from such achieved clarifications the most important American fiction concerning Vietnam will eventually emerge, or be seen from future critical distance already now to have been produced.[6] The impression collectively created by these nonfictional narratives, however, is pervasively one of self-inquiry still in process, into still-shifting relations between personal identity and literary purpose enforced — often unexpectedly or to an unexpected degree — by exposure to the war. 'I went to cover the war and the war covered me,' writes Herr in *Dispatches*, a book gradually wrought from his experiences as a reporter in Vietnam during 1967–8, the earlier magazine pieces on which it is based now like route-markings along an interior trail the completed work tries comprehensively to trace: 'an old story, unless of course you haven't heard it.'

At their best, as often in *Dispatches*, such probings toward mutual clarification in inward and outward events acquire a form faithful to the simultaneity of introspective and documentary concern. They spin double helixes of inward and outward observation, books necessarily and inextricably within books. Such narrative seeks both to diagnose and to regenerate damaged mental and moral tissue, the personal to some degree representative of the national wound and prospect for recovery. And to the extent that such injury is irreversible, narrative regeneration occurs along altered generic, as well as mentally and morally 'genetic,' lines. (At their worst, as only occasionally in *Dispatches*, these impulses degenerate into personal atmospherics, narrative means without ends, into which the ostensible subject is diffused and trivialized.) All this is also true of McCarthy's accumulated personal narrative of Vietnam. But the 'old story' Herr hears, and consequently must try to tell anew — in the process making it utterly his own even while telling it on behalf of others — is as different from (yet in some respects corroborative of) hers as the world of Greene's fiction differs from (yet on certain levels corroborates) that of Henry James's.

Herr himself, by invoking Greene's novel and acknowledging its 'definitive' presence on the way to his own violently different definition of the American case in Vietnam, invites consideration of *Dispatches* against the background of *The Quiet American*:

> You couldn't find two people who agreed about when it began, how could you say when it began going off? Mission intellectuals like 1954 as the reference date; if you saw as far back as War II and the Japanese occupation you were practically a historical visionary. 'Realists' said that it began for us in 1961, and the common run of Mission flack insisted on 1965, post-Tonkin Resolution, as though all the killing that had gone before wasn't really war. Anyway, you couldn't use standard methods to date the doom; might as well say that Vietnam was where the Trail of

Tears was headed all along, the turnaround point where it would touch and come back to form a containing perimeter; might just as well lay it on the proto-Gringos who found the New England woods too raw and empty for their peace and filled them up with their own imported devils. Maybe it was already over for us in Indochina when Alden Pyle's body washed up under the bridge in Dakao, his lungs all full of mud; maybe it caved in with Dien Bien Phu. But the first happened in a novel, and while the second happened on the ground it happened to the French, and Washington gave it no more substance than if Graham Greene had made it up too.[7]

Herr pushes the symbolic moment of violation and entanglement back through the year of the novel he cites, also through contending versions of official history, to the forced Indian relocations of the nineteenth century, into the seventeenth-century Puritan perception of wilderness.[8] Extravagant, to be sure, and done only for the rhetorical moment to shake free of 'standard' explanation, but not without power to compel a moment's intuitive belief when 'realistic' propositions are self-servingly absurd, shown to be so in part by Greene's novel of 1956.

The Quiet American is thus an active element of the passage, not a passively acknowledged influence. Pyle's body washes up here with the same specificity of place and pathological detail as contained in the novel. 'But [it] happened in a novel,' and while it is therefore apparently to be as easily disregarded as Washington ignored the portent of Dien Bien Phu, in fact Pyle's fictional death is the most persuasive 'evidence' in the passage for the fatality of American commitment to the war. It *did* 'happen' in the sense that matters here, it *was* in the same sense 'already over for us' then; in Pyle's end a true image of, if not an actual event in, the beginning of American self-entrapment in Vietnam. On the one hand Herr dismisses the novel form, and Greene's novel in particular (which he assumes his readers have read), as too 'standard' in method and imaginarily detached from the reality of the situation in the late 1960s. On the other he allows Greene's fiction to stand as reliable history of the origins of that situation.

To record the more immediate truth is for Herr to set down a 'secret history,' a story concealed beneath the 'fact-figure crossfire' of official information and thus to be sought among the Marine 'grunts' with whose units he pursued his original journalistic assignments. Within the context of the eventual volume, however, secret history is also to be researched through self-encounters enforced, in landscape of the mind, by the environments of war. In compiling such 'history,' Herr writes a kind of 'novel' very different from Greene's, Herr himself the protagonist more as witness than as hero. What he sees ('you were as responsible for everything you saw as you were for everything you did'); what he hears (listening with the same sense of responsibility to the 'small language,' as subtly as monotonously profane, of men at war); these filter, and are themselves filtered through, the sights and sounds of Herr's inward journey, and inform the voice through which he 'acts' as narrator-protagonist. Straining to hear enemy movements in sudden jungle silences turns stillness into 'a space that you'd fill with everything you thought was quiet in you.' Textual space in *Dispatches* conforms to the shifting contours of such responses, uneasily containing their unquietness. The nervous jags and adrenaline bursts of combat situations come through in whipcord loops of words whose cadences are threaded with the rhythms of rock and jazz, laced also with the terminology of electronics, and stitched to human facts by the authentically rendered speech of the grunts. Intervals of boredom or fatigue, or of frustration by failure to obtain information from official jargon, cause exhaustion itself to become the pertinent information, expressed in a spare yet 'overloaded' circuitry of prose. Initially sweeter intervals of escape to the relative luxury of Saigon, which might then sour in the aftermath of drugged sleep, oscillate within yet another verbal frequency, registering another set of observations absorbed and reshaped from within.

Greene told his readers, as much as the friends to whom he addressed his prefatory letter in *The Quiet American*, that 'This is a story and not a piece of history,' less because that was true then because he wanted the book read within a certain framework of assumed and agreed-upon literary conventions. Herr's designs on his readers, as well as his assumptions about the stability and applicability to his subject of literary convention, are different. He focuses in the following passage on the progressive internalization of his Vietnamese environments. One may also read the passage, however, as referring to a venture − obligatory for writer and reader alike − into literary terrain where traditional rules no longer apply:

Between what contact did to you and how tired you got, between the farout things you saw or heard and what you personally lost out of all that got blown away, the war made a place for you that was all yours. Finding it was like listening to esoteric music, you didn't hear it in any essential way through all the repetitions until your own breath had entered it and become another instrument, and by then it wasn't just music anymore, it was experience . . . . [It was] a complete process if you got to complete it, a distinct path to travel, but dark and hard, not any easier if you knew that you'd put your foot on it yourself, deliberately and — most roughly speaking — consciously. Some people took a few steps along it and turned back, wised up, with and without regrets. Many walked on and just got blown off it . . . . And some kept going until they reached the place where an inversion of the expected order happened, a fabulous warp where you took the journey first and then you made your departure.[9]

Absolute internalization of the war meant madness, disappearance into a mental warp to be expected, Herr learned, of those thrown deeply enough back into themselves by what they saw around them. A sense of the 'secret' reality of the war, and survival to tell the tale in a voice capable of telling it truly, depend precariously on one's approaching the 'place' where the warp occurs, travelling portions of the 'path.' For the writer retracing the inward route, as for those who more literally followed it too far, the truth of the war awaits somewhere between entrance into the esoteric experience of its 'music' and failure to return. Finding the appropriate *literary* place — finding forms commensurate with the extremity of the experience, yet capable of transcribing its atonalities — is a process suggested here as being less deliberate than inevitable. The war 'makes' for, more than an author invents, inversions of familiar literary orders, a reporter now necessarily a 'fabulist,' yet one who also denies the applicability of art in any traditional sense to the war.

The representational terms, as well as the experiential substance, of the world of *Dispatches* are thus profoundly different from those of *The Quiet American*. In the first place, Greene's Vietnam is recognizably in the actual world, whatever the basis for saying that his work has cumulatively created an abstract 'Greeneland,' like Nabokov's *Zembla*, the topography of which is finally metaphysical. Vietnam is for Herr on the contrary itself a world more absolutely 'elsewhere' than the fictional worlds of which

Richard Poirier has written. In his room in Saigon in 1967, Herr contemplates a map which, though it might figuratively have been Greene's of the actual country, has become in the meantime a map of somewhere else:

> That map was a marvel, especially now that it wasn't real anymore. For one thing, it was very old. It had been left there years before by another tenant, probably a Frenchman, since the map had been made in Paris. The paper had buckled in its frame after years in the wet Saigon heat, laying a kind of veil over the countries it depicted. Vietnam was divided into its older territories of Tonkin, Annam and Cochin China, and to the west past Laos and Cambodge sat Siam, a kingdom . . . . If dead ground could come back and haunt you the way dead people do, they'd have been able to mark my map CURRENT and burn the ones they'd been using since '64, but count on it, nothing like that was going to happen. It was late '67 now, even the most detailed maps didn't reveal much anymore; reading them was like trying to read the faces of the Vietnamese, and that was like trying to read the wind. We knew that the uses of most information were flexible, different pieces of ground told different stories to different people. We also knew that for years now there had been no country here but the war.[10]

Overlain by military acronyms, and by more poetic but equally unindigenous place names informally bestowed by Americans during the fighting, current maps correspond no more closely to Herr's old one than might NASA charts superimposing on the Latin the homely designations of the astronauts for the mountains of the moon. Vietnam is for those of whom Herr writes the dark side of the moon, what Alfred Kazin calls 'the ultimate no place to be,' and 'the World' (grunts' jargon for the US) is anywhere else. Fowler, Greene's narrator and intermittent spokesman in *The Quiet American*, is in a different sense 'out there,' like Conrad's Marlow, in a real place about which (as 'one of us') he tells us, but which we see through the 'veil' of a previous literary cartography. Herr's narrator-protagonist is by contrast 'in here,' in a place the historical and topographical reality of which has become hallucinatory, but into which we are obliged to enter. As Hasford's narrator says in *The Short-Timers*, 'No, back in the World is the crazy part. This, all this world of shit, this is real.'[11] And while Herr the reporter is in the literal sense as free to leave Vietnam as the reader is to cease reading, his argument as protagonist is that neither he nor we (not to mention the actual casualties) will ever, entirely, be able to depart.

At rare moments Herr's sense of Vietnamese place approaches compatibility with Greene's, in images of timeless color and line. With a visual particularity that must be Greene's, Fowler sees from his car fields 'where the gold harvest was ready, the peasants in their hats like limpets winnow[ing] the rice against little curved shelters of plaited bamboo,' and later watches the 'last colours of sunset, green and gold like the rice . . . dripping over the edge of the flat world.'[12] Herr, from a helicopter above Saigon at sunrise,

> could see what people had been forty years before, Paris of the East, Pearl of the Orient, long open avenues lined and bowered over by trees running into spacious parks, precisioned scale, all under the soft shell from a million breakfast fires, camphor smoke rising and diffusing, covering Saigon and the shining veins of the river with a warmth like the return of better times.[13]

It is similar to McCarthy's vision of Hanoi, transcending for a moment the abstracting power over actual places of maps marked 'CURRENT,' the quotation from Herr seeming along with those from Greene to unite city and countryside as parts of the same land, as they never really were once the American war expanded. But it is only 'a projection, that was the thing about choppers, you had to come down sometime, down to the moment,' just as Fowler's sunset reverie leads into the moment of his and Pyle's encounter with the Viet Minh.

The true terrain of *The Quiet American*, beyond the historical and cartographical accuracy of its setting, is the moral ground on which Fowler eventually takes sides in order to remain human. That of *Dispatches* is the terrain of moral as well as tactical madness — 'Oh, that terrain! The bloody, maddening uncanniness of it!' — in which moral sides dissolve into fear isolating every man from every other, countered only by those routine communal acts on which survival might at any moment depend. The continuity of Fowler's moral nature is spun out by Greene in reflective filaments, periodically retracted into opium dreams, and finally fixed in the ambiguous design of Fowler's 'betrayal' of Pyle. The quality of moral being underlying and expressed in what Herr calls the 'small language' is constantly condensed by surrounding pressure, smelted more than tempered by quite literal fire. Within this compressed field, a sort of moral life goes on, energy captured but not wholly annihilated by the inconceivable density of a black hole in moral space. 'Good luck,' in the small language of one unable to keep from seeing in each new corpse a small statistical increment toward the possibility of his own survival, might mean 'Die, motherfucker.' But the same man in the same moment might enact the comradeship which could keep him human, and others along with himself alive, for another hour or another day.

Kazin, in reviewing *Dispatches*, objects to the fact that 'No one gets above that specific cruel environment,' the cosmos no larger than the perimeter of each night's encampment, the reader thus forced into the same claustrophobic space. He attributes this to intentions on Herr's part 'not literary but political.' The political implications of *Dispatches* are far from accidental, but for all their obviousness they remain implications, generated out of material finally compelling from Herr a literary rather than a political act. It is not so much that no one gets above that specific cruel environment — how could one, Herr succeeds in making the reader ask — but rather that Herr is drawn, and so draws the reader, down into that environment, through whatever intervening structures of political presupposition. Roger Sale, in his review, correctly observes that Herr 'insists an uninitiated reader be comforted with no politics, no certain morality, no clear outline of history,'[14] the condition also of Herr as author-protagonist.

If Greene's novel is (as has been suggested) his 'personal map of innocence,' Herr's narrative maps out his own guilt by more than association — at times 'every one of us there a true volunteer.' But mappings of personal guilt, or of pride at being accepted by the grunts after exposure to combat, are not the main objects of Herr's autobiographical intensity. He carried for a time a *National Geographic* map of Indochina, marking places where 'my vanity told me I'd pulled through' under fire, reviewing his behavior like Henry Fleming in *The Red Badge of Courage*. Only as the map fell apart at the folds, however, becoming 'real only in the distance behind me, faces and places sustaining serious dislocation, mind slip and memory play,' did he find the voice for his larger subject and protagonist's role: a 'witness act' for the voiceless dead. He mourns the Marines who die before his eyes, seeing also in those 'wasted' the waste of life on all sides over many years. The book within the book, his dirge for himself as one wounded in a way by seeing what he has seen, is only the means to that end.

Reconnecting through 'mind slip and memory play' the dislocated fragments of his original observations, reincorporating eye and ear into his 'I,' Herr reconstructs his principal journey as protagonist, a journey without maps into blood and death blotting out for him all considerations of context. He speaks in fulfillment of an imperative he embodies in a Marine at Hue, 'locked in that horror . . . while I'd shuttled in and out':

> We knew each other by now, and when he caught up with me he grabbed my sleeve so violently that I thought he was going to accuse me or, worse, try to stop me from going. His face was all but blank with exhaustion, but he had enough feeling left to say, 'Okay, man, you go on, you go on out of here . . . , but I mean it, you tell it! You tell it, man. If you don't tell it . . . .'[15]

This too is an 'old story' (one thinks again of Henry Fleming, unable to articulate what he sees in Jim Conklin's dying eyes), 'unless of course you've never heard it,' and Herr is aware of both its unutterability and the fact that it has been told many times before. To tell it is to make testament of, more than to give testimony about, a story Herr expels under pressures preventing traditional modes from meshing with the subject, in a verbal rush between opening and closing sections called 'Breathing In' and 'Breathing Out.' Like the specialized language and morality of a place where 'Hell Sucks' (an item of soldiers' 'ongoing information' written on a flak jacket and used by Herr as a chapter heading), the story has become 'small,' so condensed as to contain even stories about the war which Herr himself does not tell. The most 'resonant' war story he says he ever heard in Vietnam implodes in this manner, a self-consuming artifact: 'Patrol went up the mountain. One man came back. He died before he could tell us what happened.' A black hole in moral space is one in literary space as well, its concentrations of chaos too pure and powerful to be resisted by extrusions of 'character' or 'plot.' Herr's vision is narrowed for him by the pressure of enveloping violence as much as by his own literary selectivity, which nonetheless seems in selectively improvisational control of his narrative response. 'Illumination rounds' (another chapter heading) of text burst and drift downward on the page, a reader's sense of sharp detail shown up in their phosphorescent glare enhanced by their disappearance into the mind's dark sky, represented by white space.

Saul Maloff has referred to certain photographs of the war, seen by everyone almost simultaneously with the events through the media, as 'irreducible' and 'inescapable' in a sense we associate with art. A napalmed girl running in a road; a Viet Cong suspect summarily executed by an official; a heap of Vietnamese bodies at My Lai, or of stacked American body bags awaiting evacuation; 'they strike us,' Maloff says, 'with the force of art; they are not moments among others in a stream of time – they are self-isolating and consummating, burned permanently into the memory traces, absorbing into themselves essential human meaning inviolable by official euphemism and lies.'[16] For Herr, any narrative of the war, any truthful 'dispatch' composed of words comprehending McCarthy's ring of relation among will, act and consequence, must proceed from a similar point of absolute narrative retraction into the event: 'what happened happened.'

Dispatches is of course a narrative extruded, with demonstrable art, from such contractions in subject and method. A 'novel' with an autobiographical core, in a sense actively subsuming genres of history and reportage, it resolves its central images in a fluid solution of narrative resources and improvisatory instincts. The images created rebuke the wish to filter out and identify in isolation their separate generic spectra. It plots the movement of an author-protagonist's character from a year in Vietnam through ten years' remapping of inward terrain, its lexical spaces correspondingly shaped through a decade's revision. This is so, however, on a self-subversive condition: that those who might have related it fully from experience, or even been able to imagine it all, 'died before [they] could tell us what happened.' In this lies the 'challenge,' not so much to Greene's book as to language and the act of writing itself, to 'tell it' for the Marine in Hue.

Herr would not dispute, indeed his own book reaffirms, that in *The Quiet American* Greene filed a premonitory dispatch authentic in its insight into real rather than merely imaginary slaughter. Greene knows as well as Herr that napalm makes its victims (in Greene's words) 'wet through with fire,' although gunfire in Greene's novel also providentially covers the sound of Fowler's near-fatal sneeze, as a timely mortar elsewhere saves Pyle's ears from an 'Anglo-Saxon word' of a sort found on every page of Herr's book. Nor would Herr argue any moral difference between a given number of dead in a bombed milk bar (killed actually in 1953 as well as 'in a novel' of 1956) and the hundreds of thousands of the war's eventual casualties. The fact that Greene was at least as interested in the complex metaphysics of Fowler's *engagement* as in the prophetic meaning of Pyle's deadly innocence is beside the point. So is the fact that Greene's other novels bear out this pattern, emphasizing the spiritual crises of figures similar to Fowler against ultimately unspecific backgrounds of political upheaval, rather than the fates of figures like Pyle. Witness Herr's allusion, *The Quiet American* still exerts the force of what one critic found in Stone's *Dog Soldiers*, 'an epitaph on a time that has not ended.'

Greene's age, nationality, main concerns as a novelist, and early 1950s vantage on French and American influence in Southeast Asia, to say nothing of twenty years in literary-historical as well as geo-political time between his book and Herr's, would obviously and unsurprisingly make for fundamental differences in approach and literary execution. Nor is it difficult to see that Herr's mixture of documentary with imaginative materials is in itself nothing new, or that Greene blended his documentary with his fictional interests to the detriment of neither. For Fowler, moreover, as for the narrator-protagonist of *Dispatches*, the mind is a battlefield as real as any other, and introspection a surer source of usable truth than the traditionally detached performance of journalistic duty. For McCarthy in the end, the 'fossil' type of the Jamesian heroine is as much a sustaining as an archaically irrelevant model. For Herr, however — while Greene's book is to him not a relic but a catalyst — too much of the horror, too much of 'what happened happened' after 1956, when the waters closing over Alden Pyle's head silently prefigured the hellishly sucking vortex to come.

And it subsequently happened, Herr argues by example, in ways still resisting treatment in established forms, with the force generated by the vacuum at the moral heart of the matter. 'As of now it can rain blood and shit,' says Converse in *Dog Soldiers*, in which a heroin scheme reaches back from Vietnam into California and the Southwest; 'I got nowhere to go.' He realizes that his experience in Vietnam has become what Herr would call the 'music'-as-experience of his heroin end-game. A rage beneath his words at the fact of their truth redeems the banality on which their effect in context depends. His words come from the other side of a line, or from deep within a warp, which Greene's characters never really cross or enter — this despite the fact that Greene too knows the obscenity of war, and that Pyle lives and dies within another kind of moral warp. Converse crossed the line once, on his way down the 'path' of which Herr speaks, his journey commencing in the moment when, in the form of 'friendly fire,' the world 'hurled itself screeching and murderous at his throat.' His very name suggests his failure to return. Herr crosses the line twice, once on the way to that point in the vortex where all that 'happens' is blood and shit, and again in the narrative act of returning to 'tell it,' however incompletely. And to do so is strangely to *un*say what cannot be undone, just as story-telling structures fall back into the dense matter of the war to which they seek to impart literary coherence:

> After enough time passed and memory receded and settled, the name itself became a prayer, coded like all prayer to go past the extremes of petition and gratitude: Vietnam Vietnam Vietnam, say again, until the word lost all its old loads of pain, pleasure, horror, guilt, nostalgia.[17]

As 'religious' as Fowler-Greene in his sense of the mysteriousness of his moral location, Herr is better able to go past the extremes of his need for prayer than Fowler any longer tries to pray through the impasse of his quarrel with God. But Herr's prayer has efficacy only for the moment of its own utterance. Back in 'the World' but still in the process of being 'debriefed by dreams,' unrecovered from his 'wound' — 'I was leaking time, like I'd taken a frag from one of those anti-personnel weapons we had that were so small they could kill a man and never show up on X-rays' — he bears ongoing witness in the last words of his last page to the story not yet told: 'Vietnam Vietnam Vietnam, we've all been there.'

'Imagine what Graham Greene would have made out of a particular episode in *Dispatches*,' wrote a British reviewer, dismissing the narrative as the autoerotic prurience of a 'war-freak,' totally missing the point as well as the tone of the book within the book, and in the process paying a debased compliment to Greene.[18] *The Quiet American* is classic, but in its pertinence to Herr's subject — indeed in its presence within Herr's book, and other American narratives of the war — the novel is increasingly removed from the American writing in the background of which it continues to appear. The connection is undeniable, Greene's 'information' is still good, but the distance in more than time back toward his story from a story like Herr's is all but absolute.

Dispatches too is 'classically' serious, informed by an awe at the irrevocability of the experience with which it deals. For all the jive and profanity in its prose, through which accumulate the esoteric repetitions of the inward 'music' of the war, it is also 'classically' controlled, more inevitable in the end than experimental in its style. (Is there really no connection, however attenuated, between the 'Picasso shapes' Fowler sees in the shadows of Heng's ware-house, and the Jimi Hendrix sounds Herr hears from a Marine's cassette just before a fire-fight, in the record of modern fracturings and reassemblings of 'the real'? So Mailer had found, in the Cézanne shapes from which Adams had turned away, something that 'spoke like the voice of the century to come,' where 'aesthetics met technology.') What Graham Greene would have made of it he made, in some ways timelessly so, in *The Quiet American*. American writers, here represented by without being limited to the self-shapings into narrative of his experience, have now begun like Michael Herr to make of the war what they must, in order to tell us what Graham Greene could not.

8
The Implacable 'I':
Joan Didion

This may be a parable, either of my life as a reporter during this
period or of the period itself.

The White Album

It had been an October morning in 1967 when Norman Mailer,
waking in the Hay-Adams, had idly pondered the distances and
proximities between his world and that of the 'gentlemen from the
nineteenth century' whose names his hotel bore. Thus he sub-
liminally set in motion, in *The Armies of the Night*, that active
rather than idle sense of personal summation of the accelerations
of the age which became the narrative determinant of that work,
and through which in *Of a Fire on the Moon* he converged in self-
portrayal with the Adams of the *Education*.

It was instead an afternoon in 1967 when Joan Didion, as she
later recounts in an essay included in *The White Album*, first saw
Hoover Dam, the image of which has since shimmered in her inner
eye much as the dynamo possessed Adams's imagination, or the
Saturn V rocket seized Mailer's. The dam is on one hand a huge
monument to what Didion (along with Mailer) considers a failed
dream, the idea that 'mankind's brightest promise lay in American
engineering,' a 'faith since misplaced . . . in the meliorative power
of the dynamo.' The dam is also, however, a structure transcending the terms of its own construction, an 'idea in the world's mind'
as well as a tool of specific technological purpose, its mass shaped
by history as well as human hands. Didion's description of her recollected image suggests her abstraction of the actual dam into a

system of forms and functions the value of which is finally aesthetic, residing in their self-sufficiency:

> suddenly the dam will materialize, its pristine concave face gleaming white against the harsh rusts and taupes and mauves of that rock canyon hundreds or thousands of miles from where I am . . . . [A]bruptly those power transmission towers will appear before me, canted vertiginously over the tailrace. Sometimes I am confronted by the intakes and sometimes by the shadow of the heavy cable that spans the canyon and sometimes by the ominous outlets to unused spillways, black in the lunar clarity of the desert light. Quite often I hear the turbines. Frequently I wonder what is happening at the dam this instant, at this precise intersection of time and space, how much water is being released . . . and what lights are flashing and which generators are in full use and which just spinning free.[1]

As for Mailer NASA's Vehicle Assembly Building became a cathedral, 'concatenation of structure upon structure' expressing a new calculus of possibility; as for Adams the cathedral at Chartres dissolved into the abstract architecture of time; so for Didion these reimagined sluiceways direct the flow of her meditation on 'something beyond energy, beyond history,' which she seeks to locate in narrative countercurrents of personal response.

In its scale and presumption to mastery of nature, the dam sends Didion's mind to the ends of the physical universe, the impenetrable depths of the Mindanao Trench or the stars wheeling unalterably in their courses. (So Mailer had recoiled from the rocket to 'the deeps'; to Adams too the 'planet itself seemed less impressive' in its revolutions than the dynamos spinning with 'silent and infinite force.') But Didion more characteristically retracts the impression into a moment of personal confrontation so concentrated as to resist narrative elaboration. Descending through the dam's levels 'in a world so alien, so complete and so beautiful unto itself that it was scarcely necessary to speak' with her guide, she reaches its heart, where water under enormous pressure moves the turbines. It is a moment analogous to that in which James Agee found, drawn deep into mental lamplight in *Let Us Now Praise Famous Men*, the luminous spaciousness of the universe. Didion stands a 'long time' with her hands on a turbine (as Adams 'lingered long' among the dynamos), but the moment is 'so explicit as to suggest nothing beyond itself.'

It is also briefly fraught with Freudian melodrama, though she dismisses by acknowledging its 'transparent sexual overtones.' She is momentarily a Madeleine Lee, Adams's heroine in *Democracy*, who would 'touch with her own hand the massive machinery' of society, a self-professed sensibility of 'pure steel' of whom Adams, not without irony, says: 'What she wanted, was POWER.'[2] But here, as generally in *The White Album* and often if less consistently in *Slouching towards Bethlehem*, Didion's personal absorption of the event — the conversion of 'what happened' into 'how I feel' — survives the brush with self-parody. She is for another moment, more appropriately to her general concern, more like James's persona in *The American Scene* than like Adams's heroine, apprehending the 'future complexity of the web' of American urban reality in the 'steelsouled machine-room' of New York, its bridges the 'sheaths of pistons working at high pressure, day and night.'[3]

Then, as if in denial of the power of such associations over an encounter so condensed as to suggest nothing beyond itself, she absorbs them more completely into her own persona, allowing the reader a sense of comparative affinity, but precluding extended comparison. As the essay continues, the narrative act proceeds through which she probes a more exclusive relation to American reality, the relation between a self she considers constant and what she yet believes to be the 'shifting phantasmagoria' of her own experience. The final image in her essay on the dam, projected beyond human civilization (and tonally reminiscent of, if not argumentatively comparable to, Adams's passage on the dynamo as a symbol of ultimate energy, 'not so human as some, but . . . the most expressive'), is of a 'dynamo finally free of man, splendid at last in its absolute isolation, transmitting power and releasing water to a world where no one is.' The final effect is nonetheless one of her absolutely personal appropriation of the subject, not only into a world where *she* all-pervasively is, but into a world which, by appropriation, she creates and, for the moment, commands.

In her preface to *Slouching towards Bethlehem*, essays written in the mid-1960s and collected in 1968, Didion speaks of having felt, before undertaking the title piece, 'paralyzed by the conviction that writing was an irrelevant act, that the world as I had understood it no longer existed.' At the outset of *The White Album*, essays spanning the 1970s collected in 1979, she clearly supposes the act of writing to be *the* relevant act, through which not only to recompose a self amid the fragments of the world as she had understood it, but also to assert herself within a world she tries less to comprehend than to subject to momentary narrative control. Such control is not the momentary stay against confusion synonymous, according to Frost, with a poem's 'clarification of life.' It bears more similarity to the sudden contraction, within the tight circumference of one of Dickinson's darker, self-haunted poems, of her mental impulse outward, to the edge of her consciousness of the larger world. In that reconcentration of self, absorbing at the subjective center what is glimpsed in ostensibly objective outlook — and in addition to any 'clarification' claimed — is a form of personal survival for Didion, which she defines in literary terms. 'We tell ourselves stories in order to live,' she writes in *The White Album*'s opening sentence, 'we' suggesting a community of interest between writer and reader, but the statement itself seeming rather to say that the 'life' thus secured, at least for the duration of each 'story,' occurs in the isolation of the writer's mind.

Most of the essays, in both collections, resolve themselves eventually into a continuous process of 'imposition of a narrative line upon disparate images' distilled from a broad range of contemporary subjects, all of which she appropriates as she does Hoover Dam, drawing the cultural fact into a personal iconography which then becomes the medium of interpretation. 'It's an aggressive, even a hostile act,' as she put it in a lecture later published as an article titled 'Why I Write'[4] — 'There you have three short unambiguous words that share a sound . . . : *I/I/I*. In many ways writing is the act of saying *I*,' and she goes on to say that whereas she treats many topics she has only one 'subject,' the act of writing as the act of saying 'I.' The premise, reflected in the title, of *Slouching towards Bethlehem* is that things fall apart and the center cannot hold. The central narrative principle of *The White Album* — refined rather than revised from the earlier book's allusion to Yeats — is that the disintegrations of the times, felt in seismic tremors of the self, may after all be held suspended (which is not to say reintegrated) in solutions of self-consciousness, and precipitated on the page.

A psychiatric report, based on tests Didion underwent in 1968, is accordiongly introduced early in *The White Album*'s title essay which in turn introduces the volume, 'evidence' of the compression of her sense of the world into her sense of herself:

> The Rorschach record is interpreted as describing a personality in process of deterioration with abundant signs of failing defenses and increasing inability of the ego to mediate the world of reality . . . . Emotionally, patient has alienated herself almost entirely from the world of other human beings . . . . Patient's thematic productions on the Thematic Apperception Test emphasize her fundamentally pessimistic, fatalistic, and depressive view of the world around her. It is as though she feels deeply that all human effort is foredoomed to failure, a conviction which seems to push her further into a dependent, passive withdrawal.[5]

An intaglio suspended from the narrative chain it has set in motion, this report is matched later in the essay by a neurologist's report on certain physical symptoms Didion experienced in the late 1960s:

> I was told that the disorder was not really in my eyes, but in my central nervous system. I might or might not experience symptoms of neural damage all my life. These symptoms, which might or might not appear, might or might not involve my eyes. They might or might not involve my arms or legs, they might or might not be disabling . . . . It could not be predicted . . . . The startling fact was this: my body was offering a precise physiological equivalent to what had been going on in my mind. 'Lead a simple life,' the neurologist advised. 'Not that it makes any difference we know about.' In other words it was another story without a narrative.[6]

In presenting these passages as twin emblems of inimicality to narrative coherence, inherent in the social world as in her private being, Didion elides the medical or psychiatric consequences. She mentions multiple sclerosis, but as an 'exclusionary diagnosis' which 'meant nothing,' thus underscoring the adverse relation between 'facts' and the writer's response to them, the 'story' she would tell in order to live, less with specific symptoms than with general unpredictability. We learn as little of how her present mental condition would be clinically evaluated in relation to the 1968 report. Her only comment on that report is that the attack of vertigo and nausea which prompted the testing 'does not now seem to me an inappropriate response to the summer of 1968,' on the public surface of which the Robert Kennedy and Martin Luther King assassinations, along with still-deepening involvement in Vietnam, caused American political process to run riot in Chicago. (Mailer, as Aquarius, would write of these events in *Miami and the Siege of Chicago*, in his self-portrayal there perhaps a set of symptoms comparable to Didion's diagnostic reports, if in general an autobiographical performance less interesting than those in *Of a Fire on the Moon* or – as 'Mailer' – in *The Armies of the Night*.) The effect here, however, is principally one of the writer's increasing inability to mediate reality as the activating premise of her effort to do so. Withdrawal is in this context less a passive self-isolation from the world than a drawing of the world into the self. Fatalism and depression are less symptoms to be qualitatively assessed than 'facts' essentially at one with externally observed evidence. In adverse response to these 'facts' which she nonetheless affirms as conditions of reality, rather than of delusion, the writer tells a 'story,' performs the *literary* act, in order to survive.

In the case of each of the reports she quotes, a paradigm of personal incapacitation – offered also as an image of cultural breakdown or a general emblem of existential paralysis – becomes instead a point of literary departure, initiating rather than terminating narrative possibilities, which *The White Album* as a whole proceeds to realize. Mary McCarthy had similarly insisted in *Memories of a Catholic Girlhood* on the 'dificulties' of an orphan's quest for family history as an initiating 'incentive' to that quest; insisting as well, throughout her book, on 'resistance' to reality as a form of self-creative relation to reality. Whereas McCarthy's case tends to rest on her presumption to certain qualities of moral character, however, Didion develops hers in terms of neurophysiological metaphor. She notes that the nervous system can sometimes change its circuitry, allowing neural impulses to bypass routes blocked by organic disorder. When she 'found it necessary to revise the circuitry of my mind' during the period encompassed by the reports, in response to public as well as personal disorders of the time, she also found in what the psychiatrist called her 'failing defenses' against the world a strategic mode, more aggressive than passive in narrative manifestation, of dealing with the world.

Neural paths of prose work their way out from the points of block-age represented by the reports, revising mental circuits toward what Didion calls a 'revisionist theory of my own history,' though she also calls such a theory an 'illusion.'

The adverse nature of this mode remains its chief characteristic. The preface to *Slouching towards Bethlehem* concludes: 'My only advantage as a reporter is that I am so physically small, so tempera-mentally unobtrusive, and so neurotically inarticulate [in personal presence as distinct from self-embodiment in prose style] that people tend to forget that my presence runs counter to their best interests. And it always does.'[7] In her strategy of self-effacement echoes Dickinson's 'I . . . am small, like the Wren,' which masked her utter control of the correspondence with Thomas Wentworth Higginson, a correspondence which she nonetheless also said 'saved my life.' *The White Album* shows Didion in full power of a persona thus shaped – like those of Richard Wright and Malcolm X as well, however different the contexts of their self-creations – by its own survival of an act of autobiographical annihilation.

All this may be, as Barbara Grizzuti Harrison argues in an essay on Didion called 'The Courage of Her Afflictions,' later incorpor-ated as 'Only Disconnect' in *Off Center*, a repertoire of 'tricks,' stylistic rather than intellectually substantive, through which Didion sentimentalizes her own *Angst* and trivializes her social subjects.[8] Harrison compares Didion unfavorably with Camus, Didion's 'reports from the mirror' termed 'debilitating' whereas Camus's 'reports from the void' inspire courage and the will to act. But the choice of Camus as a figure with whom to compare Didion deflects the criticism. (Graham Greene is the novelist by whose example Harrison judges Didion's fiction unfavorably, which results in a similar blunting of the judgment, just as a critic of Michael Herr's *Dispatches* misunderstood that book's relation to Greene.) Harrison expects Didion's essays to accumulate a political philosophy, and moreover to bring it to bear against 'those in power.' Harrison expects Didion as existentialist to forge con-nections between 'the personal and the transcendental,' like Camus to explore the absurdity of the human condition in such a way as to provide 'so keen a sense of exhilaration as to amount to hope.'

Didion, however, as a writer has disclaimed from the first the role of intellectual, not to mention the mantle of Camus: 'I do not think in abstracts,' she says in 'Why I Write' – 'My attention veer[s] inexorably back to the specific, to the tangible, to what [is] generally considered . . . the peripheral.' One thinks again of a line in Dickinson — 'The Missing All — prevented Me / From missing minor Things' — the minor thus becoming major things as they shift from the periphery toward a center empty of transcendental meaning. For Didion the 'meaning' is in the 'fact,' something so explicit as to suggest nothing beyond itself, which yet compels her to relate it to a surrounding reality by surrounding it with her own mind. To do so is to gain 'access to my own mind . . . . I write entirely to find out what I'm thinking, what I'm looking at, what I see and what it means,' this last thus a matter more of visual definition than of analysis. Harrison notes (to convict Didion on her own evidence of what Harrison thinks a poor sentence) that Didion has said, 'The consciousness of the human organism is carried in its grammar.' The prose in which Didion projects what she sees — 'the grammar in the picture' — conversely consists of, rather than reflects, her consciousness, *these pictures in my mind.*' It also enacts, rather than explicates, her belief that the 'syntactical' relations among images forged by the mutual impact of consciousness and fact — deep in the dam where water moves the turbine, its force in the process converted to electricity — must be improvised. Narrative sequence as traditionally understood (often as she contradicts this in her own style) 'no longer applies.'

If experience for Didion is shifting phantasmagoria, no less on the national than on the personal plane, narrative consciousness of that experience is 'rather more electrical than ethical,' images arcing between conductors in a broken circuit of self-narration Connections between the personal and the political or between the personal and the transcendental, which Harrison finds missing in Didion's work, do in fact occur in such images. But the arc of each illuminates the disconnection, even as it momentarily bridges the gap, the 'void' from which Didion does in fact report. If in reporting she does not precisely inspire courage or hope, abstracts in which she professes not to think, there is something like exhilaration for the reader in the demonstration of her will to narrative act. The sense of disconnection within (here Harrison's facetious injunction 'Only Disconnect,' misapplying the example of Forster along with that of Camus and Greene, loses its bite) becomes the point from which to realign a line of sight outward, the blocked neural circuit engendering a new one at a deflected angle. No less 'lucid and aware' (in Harrison's phrase) than Camus's Sisyphus, in whose consciousness of his fate is for Harrison the essence of human dignity, Didion confronts (not having presumed to self-comparison with Camus) the 'larger Darknesses − / Those Evenings of the Brain − ' of which Dickinson observes:

> Either the Darkness alters −
> Or something in the sight
> Adjusts itself to Midnight −
> And Life steps almost straight.[9]

Almost but not quite, the compass of the self with each narrative step seeking the region of discrepancy between true and magnetic north. Working first to reach and then to realize in words the pictures in her mind, Didion knows along with Agee, who sounded in words the visual depths of Evans's photographs, the major effects of minor adjustments in angle. She also knows, along with Herr, the importance of interior acknowledgement that 'what happened happened,' authenticity of narrative report depending first on self-retraction into fact.

The heart of darkness, for Didion as for Conrad lying 'not in some error of social organization but in man's own blood'; larger Darknesses, for Didion as for Dickinson compressed within the brain; the 'vacant sunlight,' in Didion's *Play It as It Lays*, of the 'dead still center of the world,' an intersection in Los Angeles suddenly the 'quintessential intersection of nothing' − each in its way circumscribes the area of emptiness from which personal relation, in the sense of narrative account as well as in that of reconnection with the world, must begin. To say with Harrison that 'her *Angst* is not the still point in the turning world' (the allusion to Eliot as revealing of the differences between her premises and Didion's as that to Camus) is to miss the point entirely by the margin of an adjusted angle, and to misconstrue the nature, as well as the narrative mechanism, of Didion's self-absorption.

'Every fabulist,' wrote Adams in the *Education*, 'has told how the human mind has always struggled like a frightened bird to escape the chaos which caged it,' going on to consider

> how − appearing suddenly and inexplicably out of some unknown and unimaginable void; passing half its known life in the mental chaos of sleep; victim even when awake, to its own

ill-adjustment, to disease, to age, to external suggestion, to nature's compulsion; doubting its sensations, and, in the last resort, trusting only to instruments and averages — after sixty or seventy years of growing astonishment, the mind wakes to find itself looking blankly into the void of death. That it should profess itself pleased by this performance was all that the highest rules of good breeding could ask; but that it should actually be satisfied would prove that it existed only as idiocy.[10]

Didion's perplexities are not precisely Adams's, nor are those of the other personal narrators discussed in the foregoing chapters. But each is Adams's 'fabulist' of the self, a revisionist theoretician of personal history, improvising on the rules of literary good breeding in the interest of a radical literary self-reincarnation. Reflecting in *The White Album* on her strategies of survival in the word, Didion calls them (a trace of Adams in her choice of terms) 'adequate enough performance[s], as improvisations go. The only problem was that my entire education, everything I had ever been told or had told myself, insisted that the production was never meant to be improvised . . . .'

This from someone — the past tense fails to conceal a tension, a form of connection as well as disconnection (again as in the case of McCarthy) between her former and her current selves — 'who prized control, yearned after momentum, someone determined to play her role as if she had the script, heard her cues, knew the narrative.' The narrative has meanwhile become (as McCarthy never quite allows it to) the story without a narrative — 'might or might not' — of which the neurologist's report is a model. This also from someone still trying, at the end of *Slouching towards Bethlehem*, to locate among the 'ambiguities and second starts and broken resolves . . . the exact place on the page where the heroine is no longer as optimistic as she once was.' No mere Madeleine Lee with her hand briefly laid on the century's massive machinery, she is here an Isabel Archer, in on-going narrative vigil over the failure of her Emersonian aspirations. While dismissing such aspirations, and the assumptions about the world on which they are based, as 'sentimental and largely literary baggage,' Didion's persona is not without a need, fundamentally free of the irony which is never far off, to reaffirm herself in Jamesian, if not directly in Emersonian, terms.

The American Scene both inverted and reasserted the international theme of James's fictions, James himself the protagonist in a drama of cultural contrasts played out in his mind as much as on American home ground. Didion reverses as well as retraces the national myth of continental fulfillment, from Sacramento to New York and back to Los Angeles, her movement in time and space giving over to her appropriation of these and other 'Places of the Mind.' Within this increasingly internalized geography, she calculates the 'cost,' expenses of spirit both personal and national, against the knowledge still not absolutely absorbed (hence the need to speak) that moral as well as territorial resources are not after all infinite. 'It is hard to *find* California now,' she says in *Slouching towards Bethlehem*'s 'Notes from a Native Daughter,' the history of the place a fiction paradoxically based on ideas of El Dorado and the impasse of Continent's End. She finds it 'unsettling to wonder how much of it was merely imagined or improvised' by a culture driven back upon itself, her own concern less to retrieve the reality of the place than to find something of herself in the act of improvisation. Earlier in the same work, in 'On Self-Respect,' she says that although 'to be driven back upon oneself is an uneasy affair at best, . . . it seems to me now the one condition necessary to the beginnings of real self-respect,' for which read Emersonian self-reliance. For which in turn read that quality the Jamesian heroine, finding herself caught in the very heart of the Missing All, seeks nonetheless to spin into a continuity, a narrative, of personal being. Didion perhaps no less after all than McCarthy thus locates a stratum of self in which are discernible the fossil remains of Old America, self-conceptions of the heroines of Henry James, the subterranean persistence of the type as significant as its obsolescence on the surface.

Leaving New York for California at the close of *Slouching towards Bethlehem*, Didion as protagonist seems almost to say (whatever her author's ironic foreknowledge of the outcome), 'There was a very straight path,' that certainty of obligation to self James attributes to Isabel at the end of *The Portrait of a Lady*. ('This is a California parable, but a true one,' she notes elsewhere, arguing the more broadly American applicability of Californian cultural excess, or of the California 'stories' of her personal survival of a 'peculiar and inward [American] time.') Toward the end of *The White Album* she mentions her reading of James (in 'Why I Write' *The Portrait* remains a picture in her mind), and speaks in the voice of an Isabel living on, illusionless but self-repossessing, in the improvised aftermath of her own novel. For Didion's persona as for James's character, authorial irony surrounds and limns but does not pervade a sensibility which both author and persona affirm. Didion has said of the novel as a form, inaccurately perhaps but suggestively in this context, that it is 'nothing if it is not the expression of an individual voice, of a single view of experience.' This may account for similarities between her narrative moods (if not, on the whole, the Jamesian ones) and those of her fictional protagonists. In *Slouching towards Bethlehem*, lecturing on self-respect, she had been a bit tendentious: 'It has nothing to do with the face of things, but concerns instead a separate peace, a private reconciliation.' Like some of James's later characters, whose minds he dramatizes directly rather than theorizes, Didion in *The White Album*, viewing in the narrative mirror accumulations of self-portraiture still in process, arrives at a quality of expression at once more condensed and more complex: 'What I have made for myself is personal, but is not exactly peace.'

She seems to know that illusionlessness is itself an illusion, an improvisatory state in which the writer must continue to confront herself and thus create her world. In 'On Keeping a Notebook,' from *Slouching towards Bethlehem*, she declaims on being constantly brought back to that source: 'however dutifully we record what we see around us, the common denominator of all we see is always, transparently, shamelessly, the implacable "I."' In *The White Album*, no longer needing to explain at length that a notebook of one's observations is really about oneself as observer, she refers to herself once in passing as 'I, the implacable "I,"' but exerts throughout the book her power to personalize the world, less relentlessly intent on remaking it in her image than on making her way into it by seeing it in her mind.

This is in its inverted way (and in Didion's phrase albeit used in another context) 'so precisely Emersonian' as to suggest a reconvergence in her work of lines of literary force running deep within, as well as transecting on their textual faces, the divergent forms of modern American personal narrative surveyed in these chapters. Surface storms of the sixties disturb the sea-bed of her consciousness, in *The White Album* 'later and in oblique ways,' the sixties for her continuing to reverberate throughout the seventies. But there is also the force of the tidal wave spreading at great depth through broad expanses of ocean − one of Didion's images of historical displacement − a disruption through which a larger geophysical equilibrium is maintained. With something of the inevitability of such undersea exchanges of energy, her writing registers shifts in the literary-historical bedrock, her alignment with which she often adjusts, but her occasional disavowals of which she is powerless to enforce.

Ellison's invisible man inverts, without lessening the intensity of his ambiguous engagement with, Emersonian notions of personality, making of his invisible state a form of potentiality no less than the 'transparency' of the Emersonian eye. Mailer's persona roils in Ahabian struggle with the Leviathan of History, demonstrating wherever he would deny the resonance of Melville in his prose as in his vision. Finding the Emersonian All absent, Dickinson trains a *Microscope* on Emergencies of the mind,[11] but the images are focused by the pressure of her sense of what is missing from them. So too Didion, while declaring herself 'radically separated' from literary tradition as reflective of a faith in social cohesion, renews as much as she rejects, in her fusions of eye and 'I,' the radical propositions concerning self-invention still radiating from the Emersonian source.

Influence is not the issue here, any more than it was in the chapter on Adams and Mailer standing at the head of this volume, or in any of the intervening discussions. It is simply that resistance or radical separation, like the faultlines of which Didion is metaphorically fond, is a powerful form of continuing relationship, capable of creating fields of imaginative energy as strong as those created, in the case of Adams and Mailer, by more direct convergences of voice. That literary as well as personal faultlines are among the stresses bonding Didion's 'disconnected' vision binds her for that matter still more closely into the general American literary pattern, of unsettled assumptions about the meaning of the American past. Without presuming to the comparison any more than to that with Camus, Didion as well as Emerson might say 'Our age is retrospective,' although rather than building narrative sepulchres of the fathers she inversely notes that the only 'constant about the California of my childhood is the rate at which it disappears,' her 'Notes from a Native Daughter' thus a narrative deconstruction. She deals herself into literary history, claiming as a writer only to play it as it lays, unable in the sense of ideological commitment to have 'dealt [herself] into history, cut [herself] loose from both [her] own dread and [her] own time.'[12]

Didion says at one point that 'I am not the society in microcosm,' refusing to see 'in my own state of profound emotional shock . . . the larger cultural breakdown.' But in the implacability of her 'I' she seems nonetheless to exhaust the literary possibilities of cultural interpretation through the medium of the self, at least those conventionally associated with the so-called New Journalism of the 1960s, the term itself already archaic.[13] She does so by a kind of narrative implosion, tearing her subjects from their public topicalities in a style containing the unreleased violence of the coiled rattlesnake which recurs in her imagination as well as reposing in her narrative line, and drawing them inward. 'I want you to know, as you read me,' she writes — like the rattlesnake openly signalling her identity — 'precisely who I am and . . . what is on my mind.' The inner disturbance reflects the outer in the end for her as much as for her reader, but it is also the 'subject' — the 'act of saying "I"' — through which she transcends easy equations between the inner and outer worlds. Mailer, on the contrary, seems to have exhausted New Journalistic literary possibilities, at least in his work since *The Armies of the Night* and *Of a Fire on the Moon*, by a kind of narrative explosion, dispersing himself outward in an overreaching effort to absorb and transcend not only the events he strives to comprehend but also the very methods he seeks to invent. The outer upheaval thus often tends toward mere projection of the inner. Mailer remains overall, perhaps, the more 'major' writer; but Didion is more nearly than Mailer, in the stories she tells herself in order to live, the sole survivor of a literary movement she may be said to represent without ever having joined, and of whose passing its other current practitioners seem unaware.

In this sense Didion has perhaps reached an autobiographical impasse, of a sort (as discussed in the preface) neither Mr Clemens nor Mark Twain could survive in coherent narrative, related to if distinct from the crises of personal and literary formulation encountered in the foregoing chapters — a compaction of world into self so dense that narrative response can escape only inward. Moving through the point of impasse in *The White Album*, however, she moves out into her inward space, just as she quotes Georgia O'Keefe as walking 'into nowhere and the wide sunset space with the star' she used to watch each evening in Texas, ten watercolors later emerging from that point of starlight. One might say that the essays of *The White Album* have similarly emerged from the 'sunset in space' against which Didion sees, in her mind's eye, the 'idea in the world's mind' of a dam as hieroglyphic of the history of its constructors.

Death Valley is the initial setting of her essay in *Slouching towards Bethlehem* 'On Morality,' a terrain 'so ominous and terrible that to live in it is to live with antimatter.' This is the negative terrain of Clemens's *The Mysterious Stranger* — as a treatise on morality not so far removed from Didion's — where imaginative possibilities are inexorably swallowed up in the voice of Clemens, no longer the creater of fictive worlds, now the unmaker of a 'real' world in which he no longer believes. In *The White Album*'s 'On the Road,' however, criss-crossing the continent, Didion sees America as a 'projection on air, a kind of hologram, an invisible grid of image and . . . electronic impulse.' As ominously antimaterial to Didion as Death Valley — an electronic abstraction feared as well by Adams and viscerally hated yet perversely loved by Mailer — this America is also more benignly her personal possession, a place of infinite imaginative possibility. It is a 'map over which . . . I could skim and light at will,' air her element just as Whitman 'depart[s] as air' from *Song of Myself*, having arrived in his America of the mind; or just as Agee seeks to traverse the breadth of the country in the winding walk of each sentence. Cinematically fluid throughout the sequence, the image freezes ironically in the last frame, with Didion recondensing her adverse persona and 'heading home.' But in a way she is already at home, less with Whitman by way of Kerouac or in America as Antimatter than with all American writers who, in reconstituting themselves in personal narrative, have also reconstituted the country. '*Where are we heading*,' the question formulaically asked of her by the media during the trip of which she writes, blends in the blur of travel with the sound of 'America singing' at electronic fever pitch, and echoes in jointly personal and national quest, before being ironically silenced at the end of the essay.

The literal home for which she heads, and of which her memory speaks in the final pages of *The White Album*, is a house by book's end no longer hers except in words, a personal world not elsewhere but deep within, like houses in Agee's Alabama and James's New York, Malcolm X's Lansing and McCarthy's Seattle, like Wilson's house in the Talcottville of an older time or, indeed, like a house near Walden Pond. The spirit of the place she has come to see as one of 'shared isolation and adversity,' the phrase first suggesting a Native Daughter's sense of the Western past, then crystallizing as an expression of her adverse narrative spirit, paradoxically communal in its isolation.

'*Style is character*,' Didion says in meditation on O'Keefe's paintings, attributing the discovery to her daughter but appropriating it in the same moment as a principle proclaimed in her own work as well as in O'Keefe's: '. . . the painting was the painter as the poem is the poet, [and] every choice one made alone – every word chosen or rejected, every brush stroke laid or not laid down – betrayed one's character. *Style is character*.'[14] Agee had seemed to make the same observation, even to do so with certain paintings of O'Keefe in mind, in seeing in the structure of the Gudger house a sharp definition of its occupants' collective character: 'Upon these structures, light: . . . each texture in the wood, like those of bone, . . . distinct in the eye,' as Agee presumes to distinguish textually the tex*tural* nuances in the Gudgers' personalities. As in James moral and aesthetic vocabularies fade into one another, so in Didion passages on personal and literary 'responsibility' tend to become interchangeable. In art as in life such responsibility is 'a discipline, a habit of mind . . . [to] be developed, trained, coaxed forth,' as Didion feels O'Keefe generated the 'hardness' of self and style which for her as for O'Keefe constitutes the 'courage . . . to create one's own world.'

Didion's style sometimes contains the 'monochromatic flatness' of the Sacramento Valley landscapes she recalls, the 'implacable insularity' she ascribes to the communities established there. It can also convey a serpentine menace, Dickinson's sense of 'Zero at the Bone.' But at the close, with retroactive effect for the reader looking back through *The White Album* into earlier work, the self-compositional process seems to have been like that of crystalline growth. It is more than a matter of knowledge acquired concerning the subjects on which she 'reports,' of the revelation of that knowledge (as Mailer put it in *Armies*) 'by the cutting edge of the style employed.'[15] In a sense comprehending what 'I know,' which the reader is free in each essay to judge, the accumulated narrative announces who 'I am,' self-judgment from which the reader may dissent, but from which there is nonetheless no appeal. Like crystals coaxed forth from within while also compressed by surrounding pressure, the words extend themselves into planes of personality, sharply articulated and often translucent, their precision of line residing in the inevitable yet unpredictable interplay of stress and counterstress, faultline and fulcrum. These verbal structures seem to the eye to shift from solid substance into abstract design and back, hardness of outer edge and depth of inner transparency converging in the 'shimmer' Didion speaks of as marking where inner and outer realities bleed into one another.[16]

Among her images ('indelible but difficult to connect') of a trip to Bogotá is one of 'emeralds in shop windows, lying casually in trays, all of them oddly pale at the center, somehow watered, cold at the heart where one expects the fire.' They are emblems in a way of the Missing All, paleness at the center analogous to the Darkness to which something in the sight adjusts, responding to the absence of anticipated glory. Staring into the structures of these stones, Didion seems also to regard the world from within them, as if through the 'aqueous filtered light' of the greenhouses she haunts in *The White Album*'s final essay. The greenhouse in turn becomes a cosmos, 'great arcs of white phalenopsis' like stars in sunset space. In the 'particular light' of such places of the mind, from which to remake the world in all its particularity, Didion envisions the chapters of her experience, perpetuating in the process the self-making of Americans.

Notes and References

PREFACE

1. James M. Cox, 'Autobiography and America,' *The Virginia Quarterly Review*, 47 (Spring 1971) p. 252.
2. Recent studies include Mas'ud Zavarzadeh's *The Mythopoeic Reality: The Postwar American Nonfiction Novel*, John Hollowell's *Fact and Fiction: The New Journalism and the Nonfiction Novel*, and John Hellmann's *Fables of Fact: The New Journalism as New Fiction*. Those having more directly to do with this study, however, have been representatively mentioned near the outset of the preface.
3. *Mark Twain's Autobiography*, introd. Albert Bigelow Paine, vol. 1 (New York: Harper & Brothers, 1924) p. 283.
4. James Olney (ed.), *Autobiography: Essays Theoretical and Critical* (Princeton, NJ: Princeton University, 1980) p. x.

CHAPTER 1

1. Norman Mailer, *The Armies of the Night* (New York: New American Library, 1968) p. 54.
2. Alfred Kazin, 'History and Henry Adams,' *The New York Review of Books*, 23 October 1969, p. 26.
3. Mailer, *Of a Fire on the Moon* (Boston: Little, Brown, 1970) p. 4.
4. Mailer, *Of a Fire*, pp. 46–7.
5. Henry Adams, *The Education of Henry Adams* (Boston: Houghton Mufflin, 1918) pp. 496–7.
6. Mailer, *Of a Fire*, pp. 53–4.
7. Mailer, *Of a Fire*, p. 55.
8. Adams, p. 380.
9. Adams, p. 317.
10. Mailer, *Of a Fire*, pp. 133–4.
11. Mailer, *Of a Fire*, p. 210.
12. Mailer, *Of a Fire*, p. 471.

CHAPTER 2

1. Henry James, *The American Scene* ed. Irving Howe (New York: Horizon, 1967) p. 18.

2. James, p. 35.
3. James, p. 28.
4. James, p. 14.
5. James, p. 68.
6. See Leon Edel, *Henry James: The Master* (Philadelphia: Lippincott, 1972) pp. 260–1, and *The Notebooks of Henry James*, ed. F. O. Matthiessen and Kenneth B. Murdock (New York: Oxford, 1947) pp. 320–1; see also *The American Scene*, pp. 68–71.
7. Edel, p. 276.
8. James, p. 75.
9. James, pp. 82–3.
10. James, p. 229.
11. James, p. 245.
12. James, p. 258.
13. James, p. 262.
14. James, p. 336.
15. James, p. 290.
16. James, pp. 369–70.
17. James, p. 371.
18. James, p. 301.
19. James, p. 438.
20. James, p. 462. James also speaks here, in one of several passages which incorporate the supposedly unwritten Western exposure into this record of his Eastern journey, of California as an 'unconscious and inexperienced Italy, the primitive *plate*, . . . with the impression of History all yet to be made.'
21. Edel, p. 448.

CHAPTER 3

1. Henry James, *The American Scene*, ed. Irving Howe (New York: Horizon, 1967) p. 418.
2. W. E. B. DuBois, *The Souls of Black Folk* (Chicago: A. C. McClurg, 1909) pp. 3–4.
3. DuBois, pp. 4–5.
4. DuBois, p. 8.
5. James Weldon Johnson, *The Autobiography of an Ex-Coloured Man* (New York: Knopf, 1927) p. 169.
6. Richard Wright, *Native Son* (New York: Harper & Brothers, 1940) pp. 203–4.
7. Wright, *Black Boy* (New York: Harper & Brothers, 1945) p. 220.
8. Alfred Kazin, *Bright Book of Life: American Novelists and Storytellers from Hemingway to Mailer* (Boston: Atlantic-Little, Brown, 1973) p. 221.
9. James Baldwin, *Notes of a Native Son* (Boston: Beacon, 1955) p. 23.
10. Baldwin, *The Fire Next Time* (New York: Dial, 1963) p. 119.
11. Peter Goldman, *The Death and Life of Malcolm X* (New York: Harper & Row, 1973) p. xvii.
12. Malcolm X, with the assistance of Alex Haley, *The Autobiography of Malcolm X* (New York: Grove, 1965) p. 365.

13. Wright, *Black Boy*, p. 65.
14. Goldman, p. 382.
15. Frederick Douglass, *Narrative of the Life of Frederick Douglass* (New York: New American Library, 1968) p. 119.
16. Malcolm X and Haley, p. 378.
17. Irving Howe, 'Black Boy, Black Man,' *The New York Times Book Review*, 26 June 1977, pp. 1, 34.
18. See for example Darwin Turner, 'Black Fiction: History and Myth,' Studies in American Fiction, 5 (1977) and Barbara Foley, 'History, Fiction, and the Ground Between: The Uses of the Documentary Mode in Black Literature,' *Publications of the Modern Language Association of America*, 95 (May 1980).

CHAPTER 4

1. William Stott, *Documentary Expression and Thirties America* (New York: Oxford, 1973) pp. 290-1.
2. Stott, p. 290.
3. Alfred Kazin, *On Native Grounds: An Interpretation of Modern American Prose Literature* (New York: Harcourt Brace Jovanovich [Harvest], 1970) p. 495.
4. Stott, p. x.
5. James Agee, *Let Us Now Praise Famous Men* (Boston: Houghton Mifflin, 1960) pp. xiv–xv.
6. Howell Raines, 'Let Us Now Revisit Famous Folk,' *The New York Times Magazine*, 25 May 1980, p. 32.
7. Agee, p. 12.
8. Stott, p. 275.
9. Agee, p. 58.
10. Agee, p. 239.
11. Raines, p. 36.
12. Agee, p. 415.

CHAPTER 5

1. Mary McCarthy, *Memories of a Catholic Girlhood* (New York: Harcourt Brace Jovanovich, 1957) pp. 3-4. While scattered throughout the text, McCarthy's thoughts about the relation of fact to fiction in *Memories* are to some extent concentrated in this opening section, 'To the Reader,' written for the 1957 collection.
2. McCarthy, *A Charmed Life* (London: Weidenfeld & Nicolson, 1956) pp. 334-5.
3. McCarthy, *Memories*, pp. 144-5.
4. Alfred Kazin, *Bright Book of Life: American Novelists and Storytellers from Hemingway to Mailer* (Boston: Atlantic-Little, Brown, 1973) p. 188.
5. McCarthy, *Memories*, pp. 155-6.
6. McCarthy, *The Seventeenth Degree* (New York: Harcourt Brace Jovanovich, 1974) p. 203.

7. McCarthy, *The Seventeenth Degree*, p. 314.
8. McCarthy, *The Seventeenth Degree*, pp. 211–12.
9. McCarthy, *The Seventeenth Degree*, p. 311.
10. McCarthy, *The Seventeenth Degree*, p. 402.

CHAPTER 6

1. 'To Joseph Alsop,' 15 February 1970, *Letters on Literature and Politics, 1912–1972*, ed. Elena Wilson (New York: Farrar, Straus and Giroux, 1977) p. 728.
2. See *Letters on Literature and Politics*, pp. 719–30.
3. Joan Didion, *The White Album* (New York: Simon and Schuster, 1979) p. 127.
4. Edmund Wilson, *Upstate: Records and Recollections of Northern New York* (New York: Farrar, Straus and Giroux, 1971) pp. 6–7.
5. Wilson, *Upstate*, p. 45.
6. Wilson, *To the Finland Station: A Study in the Writing and Acting of History* (New York: Doubleday [Anchor], 1953) p. 12.
7. 'To Louise Bogan,' 22 June 1956, *Letters on Literature and Politics*, p. 722.
8. The majority of Wilson's personal books are now permanently housed in the Special Collections of the University of Tulsa's McFarlin Library.
9. Robert Lowell, *Lord Weary's Castle* (New York: Harcourt, Brace, 1946) p. 21.
10. See Wilson, *Patriotic Gore: Studies in the Literature of the American Civil War* (New York: Oxford, 1962) pp. 635–742, for Wilson's discussion, with reference to John W. DeForest, of 'The Chastening of American Prose Style.'
11. 'To Louise Bogan,' 19 July 1933, *Letters on Literature and Politics*, p. 719.
12. Frederick Exley, *Pages from a Cold Island* (New York: Random House, 1975) pp. 267–8.
13. John Berryman, *Delusions, Etc.* (New York: Farrar, Straus and Giroux, 1972) p. 40.
14. *The New York Times*, 13 June 1972, pp. 1, 47.
15. 'Edmund Wilson and the End of the American Dream,' *The Times Literary Supplement*, 19 May 1972, pp. 561–4.
16. Daniel Aaron, 'Introduction,' *Letters on Literature and Politics*, pp. xvi, xxviii.
17. 'To Joan Didion,' 25 October 1971, *Letters on Literature and Politics*, p. 736.
18. Lowell, *Day by Day* (New York: Farrar, Straus and Giroux, 1977) p. 127.
19. See Tony Tanner, *City of Words: American Fiction 1950–1970* (New York: Harper & Row, 1971) p. 37.
20. Wilson, *Upstate*, p. 197.

CHAPTER 7

1. Gloria Emerson, 'Our Man in Antibes,' *Rolling Stone*, 9 March 1978, pp. 45–9.
2. Speaking strictly of the literary-critical record, initial response was less

negative than often assumed. The book was received with more warmth in England, and savaged in some American reviews (a 'nasty little plastic bomb' in the words of one). But more often than not the first American reviewers offered qualified praise, admiring Greene's craft, and seeing his 'anti-Americanism' — which Emerson in her interview calls 'mild [in the novel] compared to the [more recent] real thing' — as an issue integral to the work's subject.

3. Frances FitzGerald, *Fire in the Lake* (Boston: Atlantic-Little, Brown, 1972) p. 127; Mary McCarthy, *The Seventeenth Degree* (New York: Harcourt Brace Jovanovich, 1974) p. 187; Tiziano Terzani, in *Giai Phong!* (New York: St. Martin's, 1976), cites 'the eternal *Quiet American* as an indispensable document in the record of events culminating in American withdrawal from Saigon in 1975; and Greene, in a dispatch of 1954 (*New Republic*, 5 April), quotes himself from his journal, as if one of his own fictional narrators, in terms suggesting the prescience with which the novel continues to be credited: 'And yes, there was another change. There is a despondency of return as well as a sadness of departure, and I entered that first evening in my journal, "Is there any solution here the West can offer? But the bar tonight was loud with innocent American voices and that was the worst disquiet. There weren't so many Americans in 1951 and 1952."'

4. Zalin Grant, 'Vietnam as Fable,' *The New Republic*, 25 March 1978, p. 24.

5. Such awards would seem evidence to the contrary. Yet they acknowledge confrontation by these writers of a subject still not fully engaged by American novelists, without assuring lasting readership. Academy Awards for recent films such as *Coming Home* and *The Deer Hunter*, as well as critical controversy over *Apocalypse Now*, are similarly more eloquent as to unresolved American cultural effort to engage the subject of Vietnam, than to lasting acceptance of a particular cinematic interpretation.

6. Bernard Bergonzi, in 'Vietnam Novels: First Draft,' *Commonweal*, 27 October 1972, discusses the question of 'definitive' fictional treatment in relation to historical perspectives which now seem to have been required for writers dealing with various other wars.

7. Michael Herr, *Dispatches* (New York: Knopf, 1977) p. 49.

8. Several of those who have written about the war, including Mary McCarthy in work discussed in Chapter 5, have drawn on the notion that nineteenth-century intertwinings of US military and Indian policies are resonant when juxtaposed with the racial and territorial undercurrents of American involvement in Vietnam.

9. Herr, pp. 64–5.

10. Herr, p. 3.

11. Gustav Hasford, *The Short-Timers* (New York: Harper & Row, 1979) p. 104.

12. Graham Greene, *The Quiet American*, Vol. XI of *The Collected Edition* (London: Heinemann, 1973) pp. 86, 95.

13. Herr, pp. 38–9.

14. Kazin, *Esquire*, 1 March 1978, p. 122; Sale, *The New York Review of Books*, 8 December 1977, p. 34.

15. Herr, p. 207.

16. Saul Maloff, 'Vietnam Mon Amour,' *Commonweal*, 3 February 1978, p. 84.

17. Herr, p. 56.
18. James Fenton, 'Nostalgie de la Guerre,' *New Statesman*, 7 April 1978, p. 464.

CHAPTER 8

1. Joan Didion, *The White Album* (New York: Simon and Schuster, 1979) p. 198.
2. Henry Adams, *Democracy and Esther: Two Novels by Henry Adams* (Gloucester, Mass.: Peter Smith, 1965) pp. 8—9.
3. Henry James, *The American Scene*, ed. Irving Howe (New York: Horizon, 1967) p. 75.
4. Didion, 'Why I Write,' *The New York Times Book Review*, 5 December 1976, pp. 98—9.
5. Didion, *The White Album*, p. 14.
6. Didion, *The White Album*, pp. 46—7.
7. Didion, *Slouching towards Bethlehem* (New York: Simon and Schuster [Touchstone], 1979) p. xiv.
8. Barbara Grizzuti Harrison, *Off Center* (New York: Dial, 1980) pp. 113—37.
9. Emily Dickinson, *Final Harvest: Emily Dickinson's Poems*, ed. Thomas H. Johnson (Boston: Little, Brown, 1962) p. 99 |# 164: # 419 in Thomas H. Johnson (ed.), *The Complete Poems of Emily Dickinson* (Cambridge, Mass.: Harvard, 1955)].
10. Adams, *The Education of Henry Adams* (Boston: Houghton Mifflin, 1918) p. 460.
11. Dickinson, p. 20.
12. Didion, *The White Album*, p. 208.
13. See Tom Wolfe, 'The New Journalism,' Part One of *The New Journalism*, ed. Wolfe and E. W. Johnson (New York: Harper & Row, 1973) pp. 3—52.
14. Didion, *The White Album*, pp. 126—7.
15. Norman Mailer, *The Armies of the Night* (New York: New American Library, 1968) p. 170.
16. Didion, 'Why I Write,' p. 2.

Index